No Holds Barred Fighting

The Ultimate Guide to Submission Wrestling

Mark Hatmaker
Doug Werner

Tracks Publishing
San Diego, California

Photography by
Doug Werner

D1475053

No Holds Barred Fighting
The Ultimate Guide to Submission Wrestling
Mark Hatmaker / Doug Werner

Tracks Publishing
140 Brightwood Avenue
Chula Vista, CA 91910
619-476-7125
tracks@cox.net
www.startupsports.com

Publisher's Cataloging-in-Publication

Hatmaker, Mark.
    No holds barred fighting : the ultimate guide to
submission wrestling / Mark Hatmaker, Doug Werner ;
photography by Doug Werner.
    p. cm.
    Includes index.
    LCCN 2002094078
    ISBN 1-884654-17-7

    1. Wrestling.   I. Werner, Doug, 1950-   II. Title.

GV1195.H38 2002   796.8'123
                          QBI02-200639

To

Kory Hays

— whose exceptional talent,

dedication, industriousness

and friendship allowed me

the time to write this text.

Thank you, sir.

Acknowledgements

Kory Hays for all the help.

Will Cosey and the employees of the Karns Gym and Family Fitness Center for their hospitality.

Phyllis Carter for proofing and editing.

Aisha Buxton and Tamara Parsons for production.

And, of course, all of my students and teachers past and present for making every day a learning opportunity in this crazy sport we play.

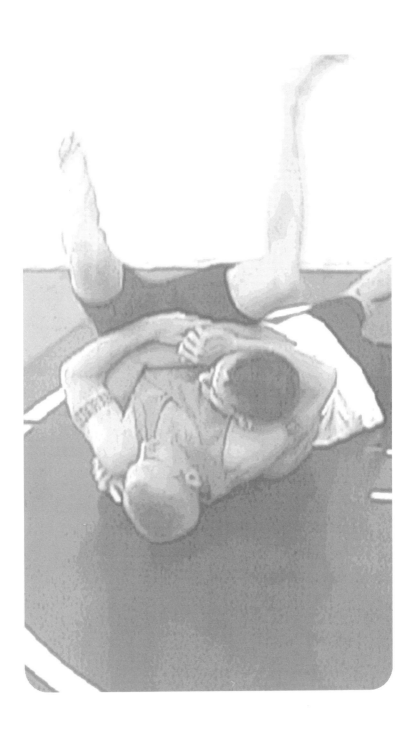

Preface

Welcome to the incredible world of submission wrestling and no holds barred (NHB) fighting. This stunning hybrid of wrestling, striking arts and submission or concession holds has been described as the ultimate sport. It just doesn't get any more competitive than when two combatants go for broke in a manner that can only be described as WCW — but **for real**.

I love this sport. For its beauty of technique and celebration of raw power. For its reliance on scientific principles of leverage and innovation borne from the heat of survival. I love the canniness of expert competitors and the true testing of skills and wills on the mat, in the ring, in the cage or in the octagon.

I love that the young and fearless can play full on and still come away relatively unscathed thanks to the protocol of the tap. I love that older players, those working through an injury and children can enjoy this pursuit because it allows one to downshift according to ability and willingness.

I love the fact that this sport can be whatever you want it to be. You can embrace all aspects of no holds barred fighting and go to war. You can play it without strikes and test yourself on the mat playing for concession holds or positioning points only. You can cultivate it as exercise (and great exercise at that), contemplative moving meditation or as self-defense and never play competitively. The only guidelines are that its expression is practical and that you are always thinking. This sport has best been described as physical chess.

This guide is meant to be an encompassing look at all the fundamental facets of submission wrestling. There is something for the novice and the seasoned player alike. So grab the guide and let's hit the mat.

Mark Hatmaker

Contents

Warning label
Submission wrestling includes contact and can be dangerous. Use proper equipment and train safely. Practice with restraint and respect for your partners. Drill for fun, fitness and to improve skills. Do not fight with the intent to do harm.

1 Safety

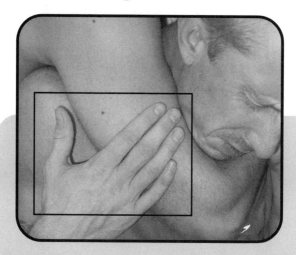

Reducing risk

Submission wrestling and no holds barred (NHB) fighting are combat sports. With that said, it is fairly obvious that there is the potential for injury. But following the basic protocols set forth below you will reduce your chances of injury to practically nil.

1. Train for fun, improvement and exercise — not to prove something. The nature of combat sports is *mano a mano*, but save that for competition. When training and drilling aim for self-improvement, not ego props.

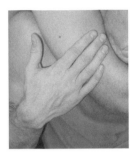

2. Observe the protocol of the tap. The beauty of working for submission holds over striking is that there is a definite, unquestionable end to a bout akin to the knockout, yet no one has to get hurt. When caught in a hold that has sunk to its last millimeter, tap. Tap your partner, tap the mat, tap whatever is in your reach. This signifies to your partner *Good move. You got me. Let's start again.* A tap is a sort of physical crying of *Uncle*. Why not just yell *Uncle?* Because if the technique is a choke, you won't be able to yell anything. Learn to tap with your hands, your feet, your nose, whatever is available to keep yourself intact so that you can train another day. On the flip side, if your partner signals the tap, respect it and let him go.

3. Use controlled speed when working into concession holds. You can fly into your setups but use control on those last few inches that are in tap territory. The difference between an intact training partner who can roll again and a seriously injured human being is very small. Respect these critical inches. Sometimes by slowing into tap territory your opponent may grease out of the move. That's fine. That's feedback. Perhaps your setup and/or retention technique were a little light. Or sure, you could have caught him in real time, but now you have the opportunity to keep rolling and find new situations in which to grow. Remember, roll not for ego's sake but for cultivation's sake.

4. Evaluate the level of the match and wear the appropriate safety gear. All NHB matches require cup, mouthpiece, and grappling gloves. Submission wrestling does not require any of these, although the mouthpiece, groin protector and perhaps ear guards are good ideas.

WARNING

ANY ACTIVITY INVOLVING MOTION, HEIGHT, OR PHYSICAL CONTACT CREATES THE POSSIBILITY OF SERIOUS INJURY WHICH MAY INCLUDE PERMANENT PARALYSIS FROM FALLING OR LANDING INCORRECTLY. THIS MAT CANNOT, AND DOES NOT, TOTALLY ELIMINATE THIS HAZARD. THE FOLLOWING GUIDELINES SHOULD ALWAYS BE FOLLOWED WHEN USING THIS MAT.

1. USE ONLY UNDER THE SUPERVISION OF TRAINED AND QUALIFIED INSTRUCTORS.
2. KNOW YOUR LIMITATIONS AND FOLLOW PROGRESSIVE TRAINING PRACTICES. BE SURE TO CONSULT YOUR COACH AND INSTRUCTOR.
3. MATS ARE OFTEN CONSTRUCTED IN SECTIONS. THESE SECTIONS MAY MOVE DURING THE USE OF THE MAT. CHECK FOR POSITIONING AND PROPER FASTENING (TAPING) PRIOR TO USE.

WHEN USING THIS MAT YOU STILL ASSUME A RISK OF SERIOUS INJURY. RISK CAN BE REDUCED BY USING THIS MAT UNDER PROPER CONDITIONS.

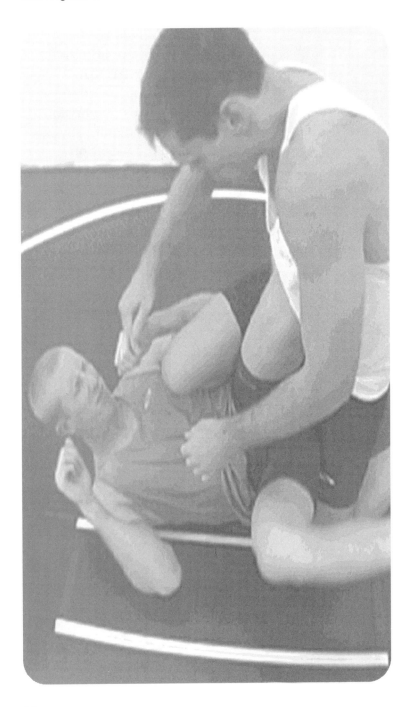

2 Working terms

Gladiator's glossary

Submission wrestling and no holds barred (NHB) fighting, like all sports, have their own terminology. This glossary is a list of terms and expressions used in the instructional text accompanying the sequential photographs. If we get important terms understood now, it will make your learning process quicker. These are cursory explanations of the positions for terminology's sake. Complete details of the positions will be given in their appropriate sections.

Arm Positions

Head-side arm — Your arm nearest your opponent's head.
Hip-side arm — Your arm nearest your opponent's hips.

Near-side arm — Your arm nearest your own body.
Far-side arm — Your arm on the far side of the opponent's body.

Base — A position of stability. Theoretically, any position that allows you to keep your hips and chest in alignment leading to maximum balance, stability and mobility.

Breakdown — Any technique or movement that breaks your opponent's base and flattens him to the mat.

Breaking down opponent from a base position.

Bridge

Bridge — the arching onto the top of the head or upper shoulders to elevate your hips off the mat.

Elevators — Elevators refer to your insteps when placed under your opponent's thighs or knees for control or stability.

Elevator

Escape — Any technique that allows you to free yourself from an inferior position or a potential concession hold.

Ground and pound — A striking strategy utilized on the ground that bypasses the concession hold or uses strikes to set up the concession hold. Usually implemented from a pin position.

Ground and pound

Hip heist — A very useful movement for escaping positions or facilitating a scramble. The hips are lifted off the mat and then moved as far from the opponent as possible.

Hip heist   **1**   **2**   **3**

Take a big step with the outside foot (here the right foot), arch hard into your opponent giving him your weight, kick your other leg over the top of the step-out leg and turn into him while whipping the turn-side elbow down to assist in the turn.

Hooks

Hooks — Hooks refer to your feet when you are on your opponent's back (back ride) and have your heels dug into your opponent's hips for stability or control.

Level change — Any movement that keeps the principles of good base in mind and allows you to drop your hips lower than your opponent's on the vertical axis.

Lift — Any reference made to lifting your opponent whether completely off the mat or merely a portion of his body. All lifts are executed with your legs, not your back. This is done by getting your hips underneath your opponent's hips when lifting him entirely or getting your hips underneath the portion of the anatomy you wish to lift.

Lifting with legs

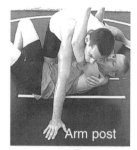

Arm post

Head post

Leg post

Penetration — Any step or forward movement that utilizes level change and good base to maneuver yourself under your opponent's base, therefore upsetting it.

Pin — Any dominant position (dominant usually defined as top position) that allows you to literally stabilize your opponent into a static position (one with little movement).

Post — Any limb or body part (hand, foot, knee, elbow or head) that can be placed on the mat for stability and/or drive.

Reversal — Essentially an evolved escape. Any escaping movement that allows you to move from a position of threat to a dominant position or concession hold of your own.

Ride

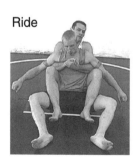

Ride — Similar to a pin in that there is dominant position, but here the opponent is moving a bit more freely and the top man is riding the opponent until a pin or concession hold can be applied.

Right sit-out   **1**   **2**   **3**

Scramble — Any flurry of movement in a wrestling match that lacks a well-defined position or technique. These short flurries sometimes occur when two competitors are each seeking dominant position.

Setup — Any move or chain of moves meant to bait or open your opponent's body for a particular line of attack.

Sit-out — Sitting on either your left or right flank with your legs at a 90 degree angle. If you sit on your right hip, it is a right sit-out and on your left hip, a left sit-out.

Stacking

Stacking — The act of rolling your opponent's hips over his neck and compressing him in this position. This compressed position takes the spine out of alignment and greatly reduces his power.

Turning

1

2

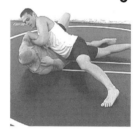

3

Turns — Any movement that changes your opponent's contact with the mat. For example, turning him from his back to belly-down or vice versa.

3 Grips

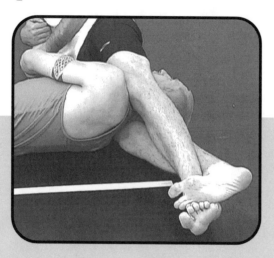

Coming to grips

All wrestlers, grapplers and NHB fighters have got to use their hands. Whether for controlling, retaining or striking, the hands are a firm link in the overall picture. Several choice ways to grip your opponent and a few ways to never grip your opponent follow. Since you can also grip with your legs, we will cover the proper form for leg grips as well.

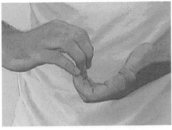

Indian grip, finger hook or fat man grip
Merely lock your fingers into a hook position and hook them together.

Palm-to-palm grip
The hands are gripped palm-to-palm. This is a very strong grip position. Notice that the thumbs are not separated from the rest of the fingers, creating in essence a stronger version of the finger hook grip. By not separating your thumbs you also prevent them from being attacked easily in small joint manipulations (finger locks).

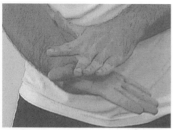

3-finger grip
A variant of the palm-to-palm for use when grip strength or endurance is at a premium. Your thumb locks around the middle, ring and little fingers of the opposite hand. This grip is strong and easy to maintain because you have reduced the gripping "handle" or "barrel" circumference.

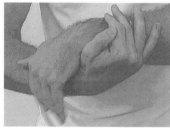

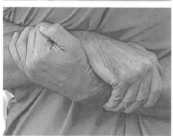

Butterfly grip
Using five fingers (the thumbs are not separated) grip your wrists. Place inner wrists together and hook. This is a very tight grip for body locking around an opponent's torso.

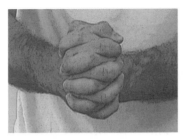

Interlaced fingers
One of the **wrong** ways to grip for 3 reasons:

1. During a scramble you can end up dislocating your own fingers.

2. With the fingers separated from one another, they have less stability and are more open to being attacked in small joint manipulations (finger locks).

3. Your opponent can apply a squeeze lock (as shown) to your interlaced fingers and cause a great deal of discomfort and in some cases submit you.

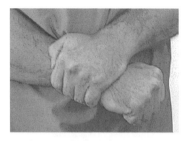

Wrist bar

Very common in body lock positions, but **don't do it**. Here you five-finger grip your own wrist in what is essentially a single butterfly grip. The problem is that the non-gripping hand is an exposed handle for peel-offs (as shown), straight arm lock setups and/or folded wrist locks.

T-wrap
or Figure-4 grip
This grip is used to secure a limb in preparation for particular submissions. Grip the attacked limb in one hand, encircle the same limb in the crook of the elbow of your non-gripping hand and then grip your own wrist. To secure the limb, squeeze your elbows tight to your body.

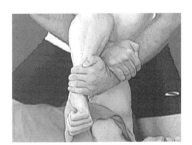

Tombstone
This is another limb securing grip used in arm-bar and/or knee-bar setups. Instead of clasping the attacked limb with the hands and allowing only the biceps to work at finishing the move, secure the limb in the crooks of both arms and then grab your own shoulders or triceps to lock the limb down. This is a very strong grip that allows for little wiggle room.

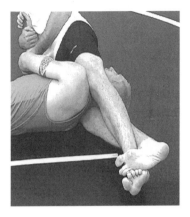

Leg scissors

This is a leg grip that can be used to secure a limb or as a submission in and of itself. Here the limb needing to be stabilized is placed directly between the knees (stay away from the soft meaty inner thighs). The legs are straight and the ankles are crossed at the insteps with the toes facing in opposite directions to tighten.

It is optimum to cross the top leg over the bottom leg and point top toes skyward. To put additional oomph into the leg scissors, arch your back and straighten your legs hard.

Figure-4 leg hold
The ankle of one leg is placed behind the knee of the other leg. It is important to use the ankle behind the knee and not the instep. By placing the instep behind the knee you are using a flexible joint that could give your opponent some wiggle room not afforded by placing solid bone behind your knee.

Also, during an extreme scramble, with your instep behind your knee, there is the potential for submitting yourself with an ankle lock due to poor placement. To maximize this hold, use your hamstrings to tighten both ankles toward your butt.

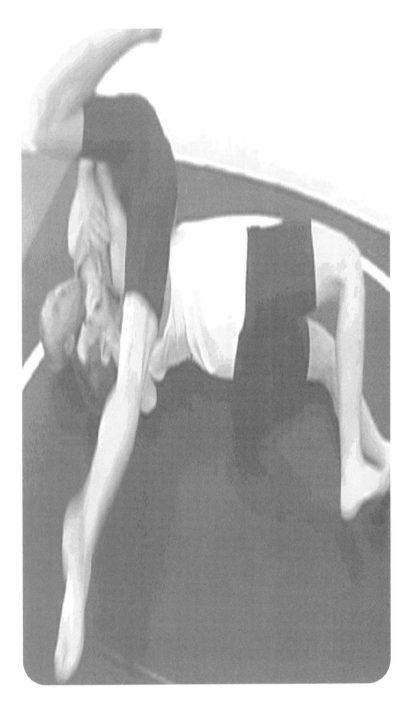

4 Stance / footwork

The key to being a good submission wrestler or NHB fighter is good base. Whether on your feet or on the ground you want to be firmly in control of your balance and optimally you want to control your opponent's balance. Before we hit the ground, let's make sure that we can stand up. This is making sure you can walk before you crawl.

Keep this in mind about good standing base:

1. An often quoted statistic is that **90% of fights end in a clinch** and/or on the ground.

2. Almost 100% of fights begin standing up.

3. In competition, **the fighter who scores the takedown wins 90% of the time.**

By looking at the numbers, we realize that we need to play the odds and make sure that we are strong on our feet to reduce the risk of being taken down and increase our own chances of scoring the takedown.

We start our stand-up game with a lesson on the stance. Keep in mind that the stance is not static although we will describe it in a static position. Once you are able to emulate the stance, start moving around with it. Be fluid while maintaining the integrity of the stance principles. Also keep in mind that the stance described has two versions: NHB and submission wrestling. The NHB stance has more concerns since there is the potential of being hit.

NHB stance

To assume this stance, pretend that you are standing on a clock face facing noon. Step your lead foot to 2 o'clock and your other foot to 8 o'clock (throughout this text the right foot will lead. Left foot leads will reverse instructions). Keep your upper body facing noon.

The weight is distributed equally between your feet with the soles of the feet remaining in contact with the floor but feeling the weight more through the balls of the feet. Your knees are bent carrying the body midway between upright and a crouch.

Looking at the stance head-on, we see that the hands are up, fists clenched loosely touching the cheeks and the forearms rest on the ribs parallel to one another. This hand and arm position is fairly good cover for defending strikes. You must resist the temptation to flare the elbows at the bottom of this defensive shell

NHB stance

creating an
inverted **V**. This
mistake allows for
body shots.

You will probably notice the similarity to the boxer's
stance with good reason. We must keep in mind the
realities of staying covered against strikes, but we must
also take into account the "shooting" aspect of the
game. This stance is a bit wider and lower than the
boxer's stance, which helps create a stronger base.

Submission wrestling stances

Square stance

Since we don't have to be concerned about the potential for striking, this stance can be a bit more open. Once the stances have been learned the footwork principles are the same for both games. There are actually two broad categories of submission stance, and again the emphasis is on mobility and fluidity and less to a strict adherence to a static form.

Square stance
The feet are parallel and approximately two

Stagger stance

shoulder widths apart. The weight is equally distributed, the knees are bent to a semi-crouch and the elbows are tucked in with the hands up at waist level. Palms face up to better allow tie-up opportunities against your opponent. The elbows are kept close to the body to protect against tie-up controls, arm drags, wizzers, and other techniques to pull you off your base.

The back and neck are held straight as one solid unit. Lean forward at the hips — don't merely roll your back. Keeping your spine in alignment focuses your strength. On your forward lean be careful not to allow your head to move beyond the vertical plane created by your knees. By overextending your lean you are easily moved with a snapdown.

Stagger stance

Assume the NHB clock position, but enlarge the face of
the clock where the feet are now approximately 2-1/2
to 3 shoulder widths apart in both the length and
width of the stance. Observe proper back and neck
alignment as well as your forward lean making sure
your head does not break the vertical knee plane.

The lead elbow is placed on the lead knee with the
forearm extended palm up. The rear palm is placed on
the rear knee. This is a very stable position with the
hands providing reinforcement for the legs and upper
body. By keeping the arms in contact with the knees
you are better able to defend the legs against shoots by
applying an underhook on your opponent's low shot
attempts.

Footwork

Now that you can stand, let's learn to walk. Before addressing specific offensive and defensive steps, let's consider some basics pertinent to all movement on the feet.

1. Always keep your feet in contact with the mat. In all stepping motions utilize a step and drag that allows you to keep at least one foot in contact with the mat at all times.

2. Step and drag in the direction you intend traveling by moving the foot closest to that direction first. In other words, if I want to step forward, I step my forward foot first dragging my trail foot behind it. To the rear, step with the rear foot in that direction and drag the lead foot. To the right, move the right foot first, and to the left, left foot first.

3. When traveling, don't cross your feet or move your feet closer than one shoulder width apart. Doing so compromises your base making you an easier target to shoot in on.

4. Try to maintain the structural integrity of your stance while you move. In the beginning it is very common to lose the upper body position while you move. You are so busy concentrating on your feet that the upper body goes to hell. Work in front of a mirror so that you can catch yourself making any errors.

Back step

This step is used as a preliminary to shooting. In conjunction with a level change, move your rear foot from 8 o'clock to 6 o'clock. This places your foot directly beneath your base. From here take a lunging step forward with your lead foot driving off your back foot. This back step places your driving leg directly beneath your base and allows you to launch your body mass directly at your target rather than at the slight angle an 8 o'clock driver would demand.

Lunge step

Once you've taken your back step it's time to drive forward. This can be done one of two ways. The first is the lunge step. With your lead foot, step deep into your opponent using the drive from your back step foot. You can also lunge step and level change by dropping your lead knee to the mat.

Penetration step

This step immediately follows the back step and lunge. Once the lunge foot plants directly after the back step drive, the back foot steps forward past the lunge foot allowing you to penetrate your opponent. To get the sequence in your mind, picture your opponent in front of you. Once you are within shooting range, back step and lunge. Your lunge foot will ideally step into and break the plane between your opponent's two feet. This penetration step allows you to drive through your opponent well past the already broken plane and take his base.

Outside step
Here we break the "always step with the foot closest to the direction you want to move" rule. The outside step is simply a step with the rear foot into a lunging step. So essentially the rear foot steps forward and breaks the plane between your opponent's feet and what was once your lead foot follows through as a penetration step.

You will see that each of the steps are combinations of back steps, lunge steps and penetration steps. The key is to drill them in different combinations to create fluidity for yourself and make it difficult for your opponent to read your intentions. A couple of drills follow to help you put all of this together.

Shadow footwork
Use either a mirror or your imagination to create an opponent in front of you as you move through each step and stance. While moving strive for adherence to correct form and building fluidity.

Lunge step

MIRROR DRILL

Here you need a training partner in front of you. One of you leads the movement while the other follows.

● For example, your opponent circles left while you circle right.

● He back steps, lunges and penetrates while you retreat and then reciprocate his offensive footwork.

● Reverse roles after a good 3-minute round.

Done with enthusiasm and up to speed, this drill is an exceptional cardiovascular workout.

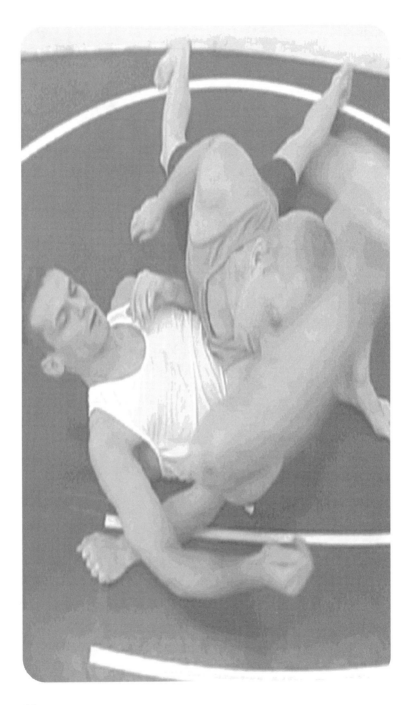

5 Gear

Right stuff
Before you roll you've got to prep. Prep is about
having the right training gear. The gear required for
personal protection is not expensive. It's the mats
that will cost. More on that and ways to bypass this
expense later.

Personal gear
If you're gonna roll, you should be prepared to do it
safely. You can get by with a minimum of equipment: a few pads and a mouthpiece should do it for
submission wrestling, but NHB requires a bit more.
We'll take a look at each piece of gear and let you
know its estimated worth to your training so that
you may select more intelligently regarding your
own needs and safety concerns.

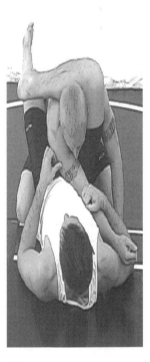

Mouthpiece

A must for NHB, not necessarily so for submission wrestling where any contact to the mouth is accidental. For less than $5 you can protect your teeth in either version of the sport. I do suggest that if you are going to play competitively, you better get used to training with one because the simple act of inserting this bit of rubber in your mouth will drastically change the way you regulate your breathing.

Groin protector

Again a must for NHB, but there seems to be a 50/50 split for submission wrestlers. Some feel that the cup inhibits their movement and/or allows for "cheating" the realities of arm bar placement. (You could argue that training on a mat alters reality a bit as well, but to each his own.) Others wouldn't dream of rolling without a cup. I'm in the latter camp. It's your call. For about $10 you can get a decent wraparound plastic model or you can lay out more cash for a stainless steel Muay Thai cup. To be frank, if you are only wrestling, stick with the plastic.

Knee and elbow pads

Your personal choice to use or not use these inexpensive protections will probably depend on any bangs you've taken on the elbows or knees in the past and/or your particular training surface. Some mats are a pleasure to roll on. Some are more like medieval torture devices with raised patterns. Some have seemingly adhesive surfaces that lend themselves to giving mat burns (think carpet burns). These items are fairly inexpensive. I would recommend keeping some in your gym bag just in case.

Ear guards
When you roll, particularly in the beginning, your ears can get folded or squeezed a bit. Doesn't sound like such a big deal, but once you've experienced it, the repeated abrasions get to be pretty damn annoying.

You've got 3 ways to go here:
1. Take a little time off until your ears are less tender,

2. work through it and let your ears cauliflower until they look like a Pringle's reject, or

3. lay down about $8 for some ear protectors and roll pain-free. In my opinion these are like knee and elbow pads. You don't have to wear them all the time, just when the situation warrants it.

Breast guards
For women rolling out there, my advice is obviously secondhand. Breast protectors are a must for NHB, but when it comes to wrestling, I've heard that they inhibit movement. There is little in the way of impact in the wrestling form of the sport so I would recommend a good sports bra that lends support, discretion and the ability to move fluidly on the mat.

Sweats, shorts and gis
What do you wear? It depends on you and your
training environment. Gi's are usually worn by competitors with a strong Brazilian jiu-jitsu, sambo or judo
background. These arts use the gi for control and offensive movement. Unless you are a practitioner of one of
these arts, I would not recommend wearing a gi.

In most cases, sweat pants or shorts and a T-shirt are
quite sufficient. Keep in mind people have a tendency
to grab clothing while rolling so I would choose something that I either didn't mind getting torn or stretched

out of shape or
clothing that could
take the rigors of the
sport.

Wrestling shoes
This is a split field
again. About half of
the competitors in
both submission and
NHB choose to go
barefoot while the
other half love their
wrestling shoes. I
personally roll both
ways. It depends on
my mood and
nothing more. A good pair of wrestling shoes can give
you some great grip on the mat, but they also can allow
for easier setups on certain foot and leg lock positions.
Going barefoot increases the odds of toes being broken
in the seams of the mat or being wrenched on turns or,

as has happened to me more than a few times, a toenail accidentally being ripped off in a scramble (yikes).

If you go with shoes, this investment is anywhere from $30 to $90. I would recommend trying on a pair of the shoes and moving in them to make sure they are right for you.

Grappling gloves

This bit of equipment is for the NHBers only. Although called grappling gloves, these gloves are meant for the striking aspect of the game. Picture a light boxing glove (approximately 8 ounces) with mobility in the knuckles and an open palm so you can still grapple.

A good pair of grappling gloves can cost anywhere from $40 to $80. Look for quality construction, something that will accept the wear and tear of bag work and the transition to rolling drills.

I highly recommend that competitors have a least two pairs of the same style of gloves of their choice. One pair is for everyday drilling and focus pad work, and a second pair (that have been worn only enough to break-in) for competition. Expecting one pair to serve both for training and competition is a bit much because training will wear out the striking surface.

Miscellaneous personal gear

The NHB fighter can always add other pieces of training equipment from boxing headgear to kick boxing shin protectors. The submission wrestler will not need any of these safety enhancers, but they are essential for the contact fighter. A good boxing supplier

such as Ringside carries all the safety gear you could want as well as a variety of focus mitts and other training enhancers.

Mats

This is where the expense is incurred. Mats don't come cheap. If you are already rolling at a gym or dojo that has a mat, good for you. But if you are training at a club level, the expense of mats can get steep. A few ways to bypass the expense are to limit yourself to grass rolls (wrestling in the yard), talk to a local gymnastics facility and ask if they will allow you to use a corner of one of their matted training areas for your club's get-together, or roll "very kindly" on carpet (this stuff burns, folks). But if none of these ideas work, take the plunge and buy yourself some mats.

A few mat recommendations

You will need at least a 12 x 12 surface to get any kind of a roll in. Larger is better, but in the beginning this will work.

Make sure that your mats are in attachable sections for two reasons:

1. Buying sectional mats allows you to expand and/or travel your mats more easily.

2. Making sure that they are attachable prohibits your mats sliding apart at the edges, which can make for some pretty nasty bumps and bruises.

Also make sure that the attached seams fit snugly together. It is rather easy to sink a toe or a finger into a seam and accidentally snap it.

A few suppliers are listed at the end of the book so you can call and shop around for whatever gear best suits your needs.

Mat moves

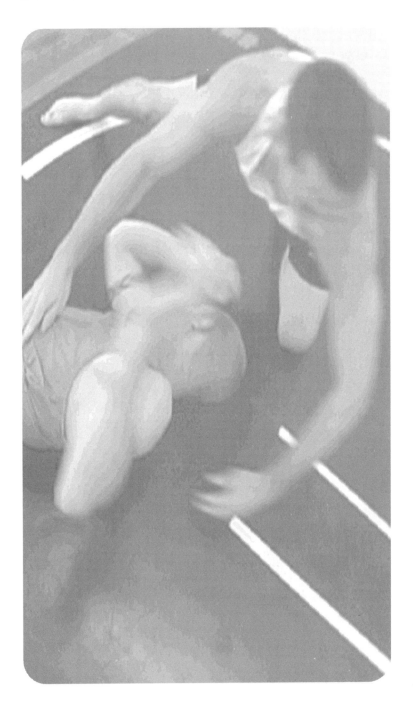

6 Mat moves

I know, I know, you're ready to hit the mat.

We're pages in and haven't even lain down yet.
Well, now it's time, but before we hit the submissions we all love to do, we've got to be able to
move. Just as there are specific ways to move on
your feet, there are specific ways to move on the
mat. In many ways, ground movements are more
integral to your game than footwork.

Don't skip this section. You can know all the submissions in the book, but if you cannot maneuver
yourself into position you'll never have a chance to
apply them. Keep in mind, just as in the case of
footwork, solidity and fluidity of technique is key.
With that said, let's hit the mat.

Bridge

The bridge is the key defensive movement in your arsenal. Develop a strong bridge, use it often and it will serve you well. To bridge, you lie on your back, place your heels as near to your buttocks as you can get them and then arch your hips to the sky.

You can either arch onto your upper shoulders or fully onto the top of your head as seen commonly in freestyle wrestling. Using your head is preferable because you can raise your hips higher. The higher your hips, the tougher you make it for your opponent. Work your bridge and work it often.

Warning

To bridge completely onto the top of your head requires good neck strength. It is recommended to bridge onto your upper shoulders until necessary neck strength has been developed.

Coming to base

The next key defensive movement is learning how to come to base (getting your hips under you) from the belly-down position. Being in the belly-down position is bad news. You've got to learn to get out of this position because it allows your opponent too many opportunities to submit or strike you.

Regaining base is more than simply pushing yourself up to your hands and knees. That would expose too many holes for your opponent to sink his hooks and/or hands into to turn you over or submit you. To come to base, first keep elbows in tight to your body. Then slide one of your knees toward the near-side elbow being careful to tuck the elbow tight inside the knee. Tucking makes it more difficult for your opponent to find holes. Once you have one knee under you, keeping your elbows tucked into your body throughout, push your hips back over the other knee. By keeping the elbows tight and pushing back over the other knee you have reclaimed your base while keeping your holes to a minimum. As with the bridge, work this movement often.

Shrimping

This unusual term refers to a style of movement on the mat in which you are on your side. The name comes from the piking movement used by shrimp to swim. A shrimp is a defensive move that can also be used to set up offensive movements. To shrimp, you must be on your side, keeping your elbows tight to your body. Dig into the mat with both feet and extend your legs to move your hips along the mat until they reach a plane in alignment with your head. Ideally, only your shoulder and feet will be in contact with the mat. It is important to shrimp all the way to the head plane, as half measures in both offense and defense are usually worse than if no action had been taken at all.

Once you have the basic shrimping motion down, accompany this movement with a pushing down motion with the hands. This hand motion mimes blocking your opponents hips while you move away from him. Just as the shrimp can be performed with both feet on the mat, it is a good idea to practice with only a single foot providing the drive. This mimics the potential situation in which your opponent may be restraining one leg. I suggest you work the shrimp and all its permutations: double-leg shrimp, bottom single-leg shrimp and top single-leg shrimp. Work these from both your right and left sides.

Reverse shrimping

This too is a defensive/offensive movement executed on your side. The heels dig into the mat and drag the body away, pulling the hips into a plane with the feet. Instead of posting your hands into your opponent's hip, turn palms facing you and scoop above your head.

The standard shrimp is used primarily for escaping cross-body positions. The reverse shrimp for escaping top body/north-south/lateral press holddowns. As with the shrimp, you should practice both single- and double-leg versions to be prepared if one of your legs is being restrained. A good regimen is to practice the double-leg reverse shrimp followed by the top-leg single version and then the bottom single-leg version. Remember to practice with both sides of your body.

Switch to base

This is another method of escaping cross-body positions and an excellent primer in removing obstructions to facilitate rolls. As in the shrimp, you get onto your side facing your opponent. You post your top-side hand into your opponent's hip. Extend your bottom-side arm flat onto the mat above your head. Go belly-down and head-to-head with your opponent. Keeping

your hand posted in his hip, retract your other arm, tucking it tight to your body and come to base as taught in previous moves. Extending your bottom-side arm before going belly-down removes what is essentially a speed bump to be surmounted if left in place. One not so difficult to overcome in solo practice, but with the driving weight of an opponent it can become a tough, tough obstacle.

Shoulder sprint

This movement is used to gain escaping room rather than as an escape itself. While on your back, get your heels as close to your butt as you can. Tuck your elbows next to your sides and bridge onto your upper shoulders. Using a rolling shoulder motion in which your shoulders are used as additional feet, walk yourself backward on your shoulders and feet. This movement is upsetting to a mounted opponent's base and also buys you room to get your hands into his hips for escaping techniques.

Reverse shoulder sprint

To do the same sprint in the opposite direction, bring your heels to your butt and arch onto your upper shoulders. Now extend your arms flat onto the mat above your head. Then shoulder walk and drag yourself with your feet toward your hips. This movement is a bit more difficult and is used in the unusual situation of being pinned headfirst against a cage/ring wall. This movement buys you some room to work with and the arms-above-head movement removes a natural obstruction to your mounted opponent's knees as well as allowing you to use your hands to push off the wall.

Forward rolls

Mat movement requires a good deal of scrambling and at times the best way to be elusive is to roll. By learning proper mat rolls you learn to orient yourself with the mat in all positions.

To execute a left forward roll, start from a kneeling or squatting position, tuck your chin to your chest and aim to place the left shoulder blade, not the point of the shoulder, onto the mat. By keeping the chin tucked and piking at the waist enough to allow the shoulder blade to make the initial mat contact you will roll easily. The right forward roll is executed similarly.

Backward rolls

Start from a squatting position, tuck your chin to your chest, pike at the waist and allow your body to roll back over your left shoulder. This will bring you to a kneeling base upon completion. Repeat to the right.

Putting it together

As with all movements, each of the techniques in this section should be drilled until they are smooth and fluid. The quickest way to gain fluidity is to link the movements into one continuous exercise. Here is a basic chain drill. Once this is mastered it is recommended that you create your own.

1. Backward roll left
2. Forward roll left
3. Backward roll right
4. Forward roll right
5. Roll to your back and execute a bridge
6. Lower the bridge and switch to base right
7. Forward roll left and roll to your back
8. Switch to base left
9. Forward roll right and roll to your back
10. Shoulder sprint 10 feet
11. Reverse shoulder sprint 10 feet
12. Shrimp right and left
13. Reverse shrimp right and left

7 Ground control

Ride your man

Submissions now? Almost. We've got to be able to
ride or pin our man first. There are a variety of rides
and we will deal with the more common ones and
ways to make them grueling for the bottom man.
Keep in mind, strict adherence to technique in the
static positions and the ability to flow from one
position to another is the goal. The majority of rides
deal with the dominant player being on top, but
this rule can be broken with the guard/bottom
scissors position. Ideally think of yourself as a top
player first and a back player by default against an
"S and M" fighter (as in strength and mass).

The Mount
(aka Top Saddle Position)

The sermon on the mount begins with the message **Make your man carry your weight ... use the man not the mat.**

This is integral to your offense. You want to make the bottom man as uncomfortable as possible. You do this by never posting on the mat when there is an opportunity to post on the man and by always driving your hips through him.

This position is broken into four sub-positions: heel back/grapes in, high and tight, knee mount and big brother. We will start with the first and work our way up the body.

Heel back / grapes in

● You are lying on top of your opponent with your hips arched through him and either

● a) with your heels hooked back between his legs arching to the ceiling and squeezing your knees together or

● b) with your heels hooked between his legs and your insteps "grape-vined" around his shins spreading his legs apart. Either leg position creates a good deal of pressure on an opponent's lower body.

● Stabilize the upper body by either

● a) sandwiching your opponent's head between your forearms and applying pressure (be sure to sandwich at the ear to take advantage of maximum leverage and discomfort) or

● b) by hooking his head deep into the crook of one arm driving your shoulder hard across his face and using your other hand to underhook an arm and separate it from his body, preferably taking it above the plane of his shoulders.

High and tight

● This position assumes your opponent has beat your lower body control (released the grapes and/or beat the heel back) making it difficult for you to keep your hips through, and easy for him to bridge.

● Using his head as a handle (use whatever hand is already behind his head) pull yourself up his body until you are sitting on his chest with your knees jammed tight into his armpits.

● Keep his head lifted off of the mat to beat the bridge and keep your weight settled on his chest (not on your knees). You will be pinching your knees together throughout.

Knee mount

● This and big brother are not fall back positions. Hit these to strengthen your position and create even more discomfort for your opponent.

● Place the shin of one of your mounted legs onto your opponent's chest. Point your knee at a diagonal angle across his chest. Sink your weight into him and pinch in tight with the grounded knee. Compression on the heart and lungs of your opponent causes a great deal of discomfort.

● It also affords better punching power for the NHB game and the ability to move more quickly in a scramble. If your opponent were to bridge in the diagonal direction of the riding knee, it would drive your knee through his jaw at the height of his bridge. Pretty sweet. If he were to bridge in the opposite direction, your knee would cross back to the high and tight.

Big brother

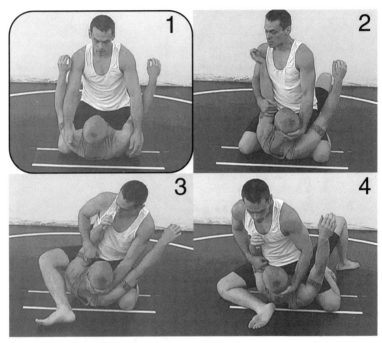

● We look at moving into big brother from the high and tight position.

● With your knees tight into his armpits, raise one of his arms off of the mat and step your right leg around until you are based on the outside of that calf.

● Lean toward that calf and step the other leg around. From here, lean over your opponent's head, use your heels for base into the mat, and squeeze your knees together. You can lift his head off the mat to add to his discomfort.

MOUNT DRILL: Mount Climber

I suggest you work on chaining the mount moves to learn them properly.

● Start with the heel back / grapes-in.
● Move on to high and tight.
● Hit the right knee mount.
● Settle back into high and tight.
● Set up big brother by stepping the right leg around first.
● Climb back down the body in the same sequence and repeat, this time hitting the knee mount and big brother from the left side.

Cross-body

There are many ways to hit the cross-body position, which is you in top position lying perpendicular to your opponent. Here are two high percentage ways to establish the cross-body. These positions are easy to defend and provide excellent opportunities to strike and seek submissions.

Cross-body ride

● This is the bread and butter of the cross-body game.

● Here you place yourself chest to chest with your opponent at a perpendicular angle. Do not ride yourself more than mid-sternum across your opponent's mid-sternum or you will be increasing your opponent's chances of bridging and rolling you.

● Keep your hips low to the mat and stay off your knees throughout. This increases the load your man is carrying.

● Dig your toes into the mat to give more power to your hips arching through your man.

Hip cut

● An addition to the cross-body ride that provides the opportunity to defend against your man's attempts to place you in guard or half guard.

● As he attempts to bring the bottom knee through to guard, cut the hip-side point of your pelvis to the mat to block his move.

● By successfully training the hip cut to retain your opponent, you leave your hands free to execute strikes and/or set up submissions.

Also by going hands-free you will be more likely to flow freely on top of your opponent rather than use static strength retention.

CROSS-BODY DRILL:
Rock around-the-clock

● While lying across your opponent's body, visualize him as a clock
face with his far hip as 12 o'clock,
his near hip as 6, his head as 9, and
his feet as 3.

● Practice flowing in the cross-body
ride by clocking yourself back and
forth from the 6 to 12 o'clock positions, around his head.

● By avoiding passing the 3 o'clock
position or feet, you limit his opportunity to attempt to guard you and
defend with his legs.

● While working the clock be sure to
maintain proper sternum position,
keep your hips low and stay off your
knees throughout.

Head and arm position

1

2

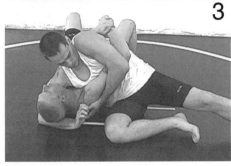

3

This ride, also known as a scarf hold in some circles, is a variant of the cross-body.

● Your far-side arm encircles your opponent's head and your near-side arm clasps his near triceps and pulls it tight into you and away from his body.

● You will sit out on your hip-side hip and kick your sit-out thigh underneath his near shoulder. This acts as a kickstand and prevents his bridge and roll. Keep your head low and into him to prevent him from wedging his far arm into your neck and pushing you off. If possible, keep his head turned away from your body making it harder for him to work his counters.

4

● You want your hips to be off the mat and pulling away from his shoulders at a perpendicular angle. This increases the amount of weight he has to carry.

5

6

Moving into head and arm from cross-body ...

● From the cross-body position, first set your hands in proper head and arm position (encircling the head or clasping the near arm, etc.) and then perform your sit-out.

... and vise versa

● To move from head and arm to cross-body, step your sit-out leg into hips-down position and then release the hand positions.

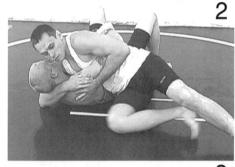

Top body hold / lateral press
(aka North / South and 69)

In this position, you maneuver your body head-to-head with your opponent and essentially observe the mechanics of the cross-body ride: sternum-to-sternum cohesion, hips driving through and staying off your knees. You also have the bonus of being able to apply your hip cuts directly to an opponent's head.

Your arms are in tight to his sides, squeezing in and dragging back against his armpits with your elbows while your hands hook his waistband or short ribs. Work this position in the Rock Around-the-Clock drill.

Working back and forth from the top body hold and head and arm position require a bit more technique.

Moving into top body from head and arm ...

● From the head and arm position, step your outside leg far across your opponent's face into the 45 degree hole above your opponent's far shoulder.

● Transfer your hips across his face while releasing your head and arm hand position and acquiring the top-body hold hand position. Keep your hips low and your weight driving throughout. To move from top-body to head and arm, clock to a cross-body ride and then work into your head and arm position from there.

... and vise versa

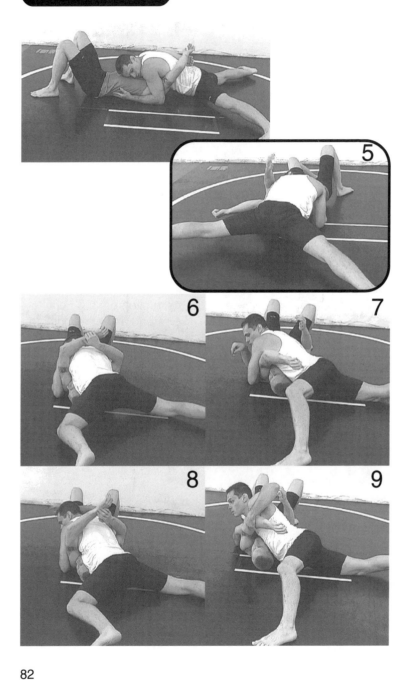

Moving into the mount from cross-body

There are essentially two ways to hit the top saddle/mounted position from the cross-body ride.

Knee sneak

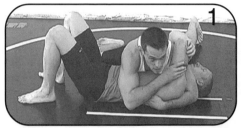

● Sneak your hip-side knee onto your opponent's stomach and seek to drive it across until it meets the mat on the opposite side attaining the mount.

● This is OK during a scramble but any other time it has the drawback of taking weight off your man. Once you place your knee on the bottom man's stomach, you have no choice but to alleviate the pressure of your ride giving a skilled opponent opportunity to escape.

● It is for this same reason that we do not advocate the position known as the knee ride or knee-on-stomach/knee-on-chest position. Your base rides too high and the exploded position allows too much room for the bottom man to work.

High leg over

● This is a safer way to attain the mount. You merely sit out on your head-side hip (you will be facing his hips). From there step what is now your outside leg across his body onto the mat.

● Your stepped foot will hook into his far leg as if spurring a horse while you pull your body on top of him. This is a ballistic, dynamic movement. If not set up properly you allow your opponent the opportunity to defend with his legs placing you in half or full guard.

● The best setup is an overbearing crossbody ride that has already drained the bottom man. Apply a short elbow dig into the femoral mass (the soft meaty tissue of the inner thigh) of his near thigh just before your ballistic stepover.

Mounting strategy

The mount is indeed a dominant position, but it isn't the only one. Between two skilled players, the game of positioning is more likely to be one of see-sawing cross-body and top-body rides rather than exchanged mounts. Don't get me wrong, the mount is great — just don't bypass all the striking and sub-mission opportunities available along the way.

Guard / bottom scissors position

This is the one position in which being on your back can be an opportunity for victory. With that said, I strongly advocate playing off your back only as a position of default. If you are playing an aggressive S & M (strength and mass) fighter you may have no choice but to hit your back. If you must let's make sure you can do it safely. There are four guard variants. We'll look at them in sequence.

From inside out ...

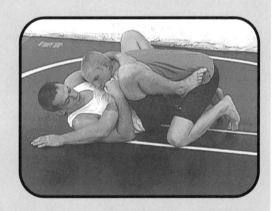

Closed guard

● Control is achieved by wrapping your legs around your opponent's body. Some schools of thought advocate crossing the legs at the ankles, which is not bad for fluid movement, but can be a blessing to the man inside your guard if he is a good leg locker.

● I recommend you work your closed guard from a leg Figure-4 position. This makes your legs more secure against locking, and you can apply a mightier squeeze increasing your opponent's level of discomfort.

Another view ...

● Control his head with one hand on the back of his neck. Keep in mind that if he is able to get his head up and away from you, he is free to strike and/or shoot for leg locks.

● Overhook an arm deeply at the arm pit to control another striking tool. This gives you better leverage to keep him from sitting back on you. This head and arm tie-up position also provides numerous submission setups.

● Use the elbow of your head-controlling arm to elevate his free arm. Insert your same-side knee into the space created by this elevation. Keep your elbow tucked inside this knee to block strikes from the free hand. Keep the foot of your blocking knee tight in his hip.

Open guard

● You are on your back but are unable or unwilling to close your legs around your opponent. Plant your feet in your opponent's hips to control him with short extensions of your legs. Keep your knees squeezed tight into him to prevent his "passing" your guard easily.

● As with the closed guard position, you want to seek a head and arm tie-up. You have submissions and turnovers available here, and you are also a bit more mobile than in the stalemate of the closed guard.

● A warning: some practitioners work the open guard with their insteps hooked underneath their opponent's inner thighs. This is fine for work in which leg locks have been limited to particular straight-leg classes, but a huge mistake otherwise. There are simply too many opportunities for a good leg lock artist to work from this position.

Top scissors / inside guard position

Now we address what you do inside your opponent's legs. This is a time that being in top position can be dangerous. We cover escapes from this position later (called guard passing by many). Here is one way to ride this position making it uncomfortable for your man, reducing his submission chances and providing you with opportunities to set up leg locks.

Sprawl

● Ride as in the cross-body ride. Keep your hips low and driving, stay off your knees and keep your arms clamped tight to his sides.

● By keeping your hips low and tight you are able to prevent his setting up arm bars and/or turnovers.

● On each of your opponent's offensive attempts, hip cut into the thigh working for the most mobility. You may be able to slither over the top of a thigh trapped by a hip cut.

Back rides

Gaining your opponent's back is a very powerful position. We will explore three ways to ride.

Hooks in

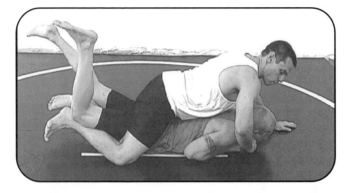

● Sink your heels deep into your opponent's hips.

● Arch your pelvis through his lumbar spine and control his head or at least one arm. It is optimum to control both one arm and his head.

Cockle-burr

● Here the opponent keeps his hips down preventing you from getting your hooks in.

● Hook your insteps over the inside of his legs approximately 6 inches below the knees and spread his legs out hard.

● Drive your hips through and control the head or arms.

Highball ride

● When you are able to get only one hook in, sink it deep and hit a Figure-4 leg grip. Arch your hips through hard.

● Control the head and or arm(s) as in the previous rides.

● It is important to keep your hips on top of your opponent during the highball instead of off to the side in order to create more pressure.

Ground control

BACK DOOR MAN DRILL

● Use this drill to train back rides.

● Start with a cockle-burr ride. Allow your partner to bring his knees under him to return to base and hook your left leg in for a left highball ride.

● Hook your other leg in for a hooks in ride, pop your left leg out and hit a right highball ride.

● Pop your right leg out and then restart the drill. Drill for 3, 3-minute rounds alternating positions with the bottom man.

This ends the basics of positioning and drills to make them solid. Now it's time to talk about getting your man down.

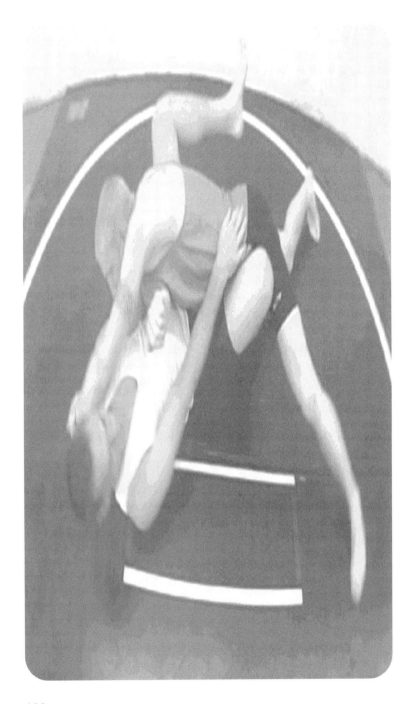

8 Takedowns

Down and out
It's finally here — it's time to fight.

To take someone down you must adhere to all of
the principles covered in the stance and footwork
section as well as adding the following idea to the
mix. **If you can't touch the man, don't shoot**.
Keep this first and foremost in your mind when setting up any shot.

In submission wrestling, this means shooting only
when you can reach out and touch your opponent.
In NHB this means shooting only when you can
stick him with a jab. To shoot from anywhere
beyond your arm's length gives him too much time
to react, defend and counter.

There are numerous ways to take someone down. There are variations upon variations. But all variations start with root techniques — techniques that are the bread and butter of dropping another human.

Instead of explaining a random series of takedowns or laboring one takedown through all of its permutations, we chose the fundamentals of six varieties to give you a well-rounded palette of drops. With a little experimentation, these will serve you well.

So it's up to your creativity. Just as it is in creating sensible boxing combinations where you have only a few punches, but oh so many ways to put them together, the same can be said for the following shots.

Double leg

The first and most important shot to learn is the double leg. You can hit this move standing or while hitting a knee to the mat. First the standing version.

● Make sure you can touch your man!

● Back step, level change and execute a penetration step.

● While penetrating, be sure that your shoulders do not extend beyond the vertical plane of your knees.

● Hit him where he bends. This means hands behind each knee (not on his hamstrings) and your shoulder into his hip. Hitting someone where he bends makes him vulnerable.

● Now drive. Once you are in on any takedown, think of it as a 50-yard dash where someone happens to be in front of you.

High single leg

Not the ultimate that a good double leg is but still effective.

● Snatch directly behind his lead knee with your inside hand. Snatching with the outside hand allows your opponent to hit a wizzer.

● Follow with your outside hand and lock your hands directly behind his knee.

● Grip the hands palm-to-palm with the outside hand on top. This prevents him from pulling them apart easily.

● Place your head in one of two positions:

1. Head in ribs.
2. Head to the inside with your biceps and shoulder on top of his thigh.

● Drive!

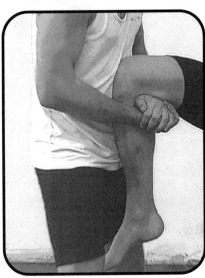

Low single leg

A very effective shot not often seen in mixed martial arts competition outside of Japan.

● Make sure that you can touch your man.

● Back step, level change and execute a penetration step.

● Hit both knees to the mat.

● The inside hand reaches first followed by the outside hand to cup his heel.

● Keep your head to the inside of his leg placing your outside shoulder against his shin.

● Drive.

Hip toss

A powerful and dynamic takedown performed from the over-underhook position.

● Establish an over-underhook. This entails you underhooking his armpit on one side and overhooking his arm on the other. Keep your head and most of your weight on the overhook side. Be aware that while in this position your opponent has the same offenses available to him.

● Get your opponent circling toward your underhook side.

● Back step your hips into his while bending your knees.
● Straighten your legs to lift his feet off the mat.
● Pull down on your overhook side and lift up on your underhook side.

Crunch

A good bread and butter takedown from the body lock (bear hug) position.

● Grip your hands around his lower back.

● Pull him tight to you while you use your shoulder or head to drive into his chest.

● You are able to easily step into a mounted position from here.

A closer look ...

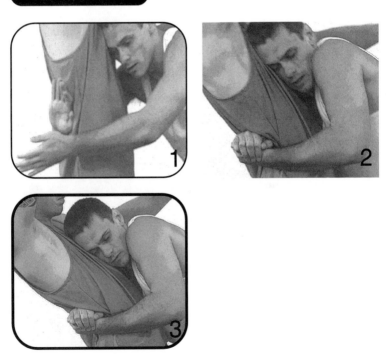

Headlock throw

An effective technique to use from the head and arm tie-up position. The head and arm tie-up is where you have one hand controlling your opponent's neck and your other arm controlling your opponent's neck-controlling hand at the elbow.

● Pull his head to you.
● Keep his arm tight to you.
● Back step your hips into him while bending at the knees.
● Once he is pulled tight onto your hip, straighten your knees to lift him off the mat.
● Pull down on his arm and head and bend deep at the waist to finish.

9 Takedown defense

Staying on your feet
There are many, many ways to get dropped. Getting dropped hurts. We will discuss a few ways to keep from going down and how to end up on top if you do.

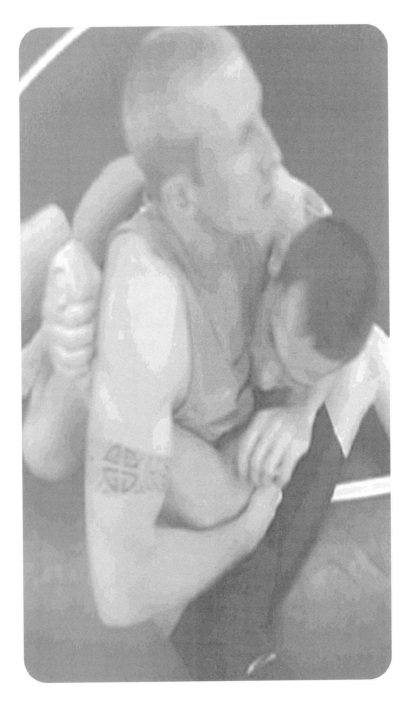

Range

One of the best ways to keep from going down is to play outside your opponent's shooting range. We know from the takedown chapter that to shoot intelligently you've got to be able to touch your opponent. Thus you must realize that if you are close enough to shoot, you are close enough for an opponent to take a shot at you.

In NHB you can use the jab, stick him and constantly move to upset his takedown plans. In pure submission wrestling, it's a dance of closing the range for your shot attempts and opening the range for your opponent's attempts.

Working rounds with a partner where each of you takes turns going for the shot while the other opens the range is excellent training.

Level change

Once you are playing at the edge of shooting range, be ready to match your opponent's level change. You can only be taken down if he gets his hips under you. When you match his level of entry you reduce his odds of getting his hips in proper position.

Working the level change component, which must be present in all of the following defenses, is good training with a partner. You will each initiate a shot accompanied by a level change. These shots can be incomplete, merely setting up for the shot. Your job is to react to the initiation by dropping your base to match his level change.

Switch step

In range defense you maintain the integrity of your stance and play to the outside of shooting distance. The switch step is used when you may be in a little closer than you realize or your opponent's shot was fast (and trust me, shots can come like Vin Diesel, fast and furious).

The switch step is nothing more than a stance shift, stepping your lead foot to the rear removing it as a target for the attempted shot. To drill it, as your partner shoots for your lead leg, attempt to switch step before he can hook it. This step must be a ballistic step — you can't switch step slowly.

Bull post

We've been working takedown defenses from the outside in. Here you are in range and it's a bit late for the switch step. Lower your base and post your hands on the opponent's shoulders. This stops his bull's rush.

It is vital that you change levels with his shot to be effective with the bull post. If his level is lower than yours, he will be able to crash right through your arms and complete the shoot. Change levels and the move is yours.

Sprawl

The sprawl must be mastered for you to be successful at this game. Your opponent has shot with a good level change. To defend this, sprawl (flatten) your hips into him.

There is specific technique to be observed here:

● Try to sprawl your hips into his head and not further down his back. To do so allows him the opportunity to drag your hips in and drop you.

● Sprawl at an angle to reduce his drive through you.

● Once you sprawl you can keep you hips squared into him or hit a series of hip cuts to further stabilize your position.

● Keep your hips arched through your opponent at all times.

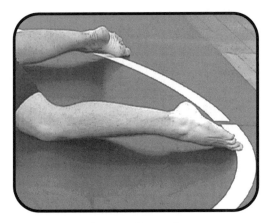

● Keep your insteps flat to the mat once you sprawl. There is a temptation to dig in with the toes, but if your opponent continues to drive, your strong toe position will allow your opponent to drive your hip level higher. With the insteps-flat position, you will merely slide along the mat in your original sprawl position as your opponent continues to drive.

Wizzer

The wizzer is used primarily against single leg and double leg takedowns that are not properly set up.

● Overhook your arm deep into the armpit of your opponent's outside attacking arm.

● Lever your whole body into the overhook arm turning around it as if it were a hinge.

● Keeping your weight through your opponent, drive your wizzer shoulder to the mat. This brings his captured shoulder down.

Another view ...

Forearm wedge

A last-ditch contingency defense against the hip, shoulder and head lock throws. You have been caught, your feet are lifted and it's too late for the hip block.

● Insert your free forearm across your opponent's back with your palm facing you.

● Push with your forearm and attempt to ride your hips around during the throw to remain on your feet.

Base break

A closer view ...

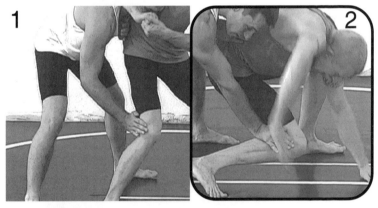

A very easy way to stop head lock throws.

● Simply post your far-side hand on his near knee at a downward 45-degree angle to break his base.

Sag

This is the "go-to move" when your opponent hits any front body lock (bear hug) position. You've got to hit it fast to stop any salto/suplex throws.

● Sag your hips away immediately. This involves taking your hips away from him and giving him as much weight as you can afford with your upper body.

5

● Use one or both of your hands to drive his chin back at an angle.

These are good, solid strategies and techniques to keep you on your feet when you want to be there. You have to drill all takedowns and their counters in live action. Begin working with a partner learning the techniques as well as you can in a slow and controlled fashion. Then turn up the heat and make honest efforts to take one another down while the other counters the shots. It's the only way to make sure you're ready to roll.

10 Submissions

Enough already!

It's time to start tapping. We will look at a variety of submissions from all positions. I hope you studied the previous sections well, because if you can't ride your man, you can't hook him.

There are innumerable submissions floating around out there, but we will cover only the highest percentage moves. Get these hooks down pat and you are well on your way to being formidable.

Mount submissions

We'll work up the body in the four mounted positions illustrating top dog submissions for each.

Heel back shin lock

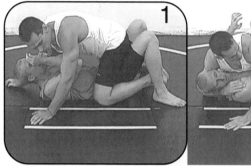

● From the heel-back position, attack his right leg by cutting into him with your right hip.

● Angle your body to your right and extend your left leg toward his right side retaining his caught right leg with your instep.

● Grab his right toes with your left hand and twist his foot over your extended left leg to tap.

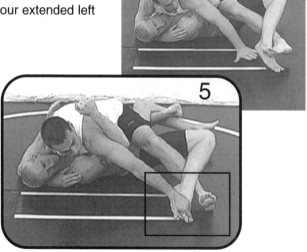

Heel back neck lock

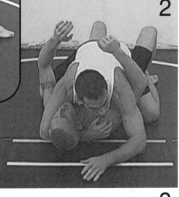

● From the heel-back position, wrap your right arm around the back of his neck.

● Position his chin on top of your right shoulder.

● Place your right hand on your left biceps in a lever grip.

● Grip the back of your neck with your left hand.

● Squeeze your elbows together while arching your back and extending his legs away from him with your grapes to tap.

Half nelson pry

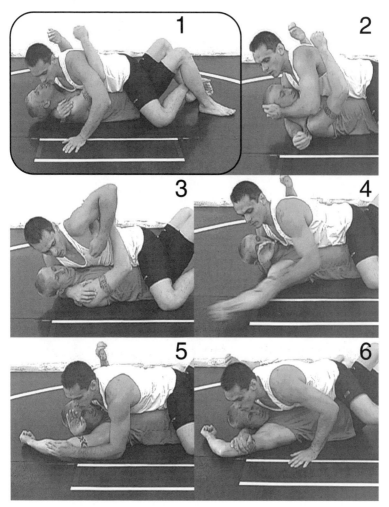

● From the heel-back position, wrap your right arm around the back of his neck.

● Take his right arm away from his body and over his head with your left arm.

● Grip his right arm at the elbow with your right hand.

● Straighten your right arm while arching your right shoulder through his head.

● Reach under his head and grab the back of it with your left hand.

● Lever his chin toward his chest to tap.

Falling full arm bar

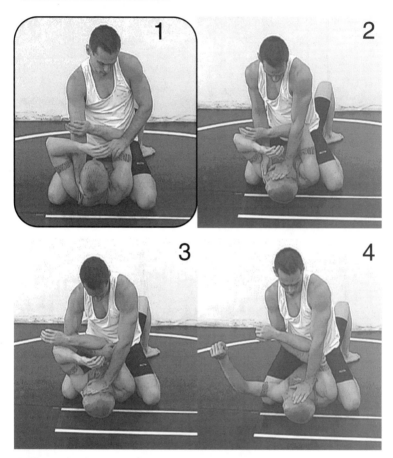

● From the high and tight position, place your left hand on his face and put all of your weight through his head.

● Grip his right arm at the biceps with your right hand pulling his arm tight to your body.

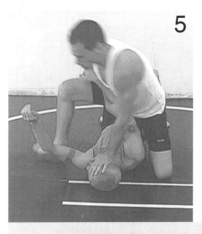

5

● Leaning all of your weight through your left hand and using that hand as a pivot point, swing your left leg around and over the top of his head.

● Fall to your left onto your back retaining his right arm. You are now lying perpendicular to your opponent.

6

7

● Your legs will be straight and extended across him, your left leg across his face, your right across his body.

● Squeeze your knees together, pull his hand tight to your chest and arch your hips to the sky to tap.

Top wrist lock

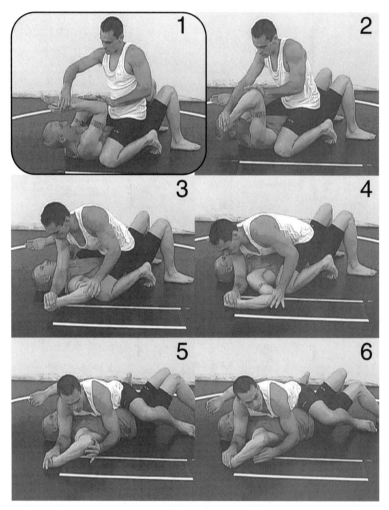

● From the knee mount position, your right hand grabs his right hand and your left palm is positioned at his right elbow.

● Use your left palm to drive his arm over his head to his right and onto the mat. This is a set-up move to beat an opponent's natural resistance to you forcing his arm to the mat.

● Drop your weight from a knee mount to a heel back.

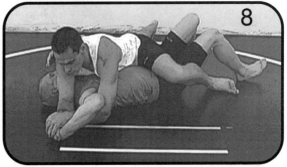

● Place your left arm underneath his right arm and grip on top of your right hand that is still holding his right hand.

● Release your right grapevine and sprawl toward your right while hooking his hip-hand with your left leg.

● Pull your elbows tight to his body.

● Twist his right hand as if throttling a motor-cycle and squeeze your elbows together tight to tap.

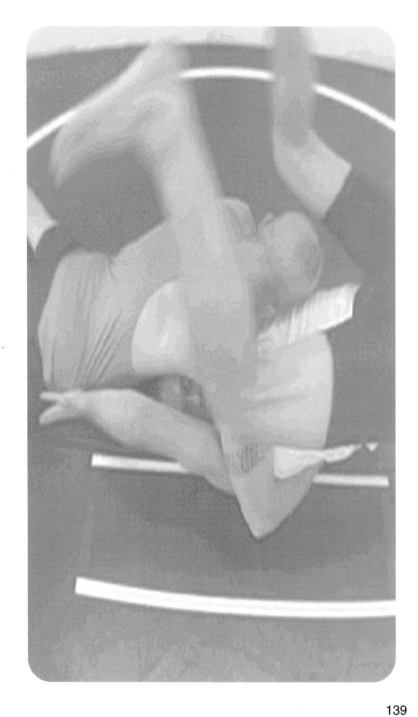

Cross-body submissions

Top wrist lock

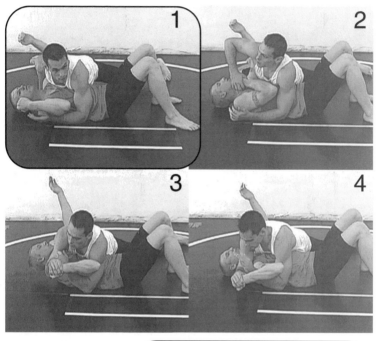

● This is the cross-body version of a movement from the mounted position.

● Use your head-side hand (here the right) to grab his right hand.

● Reach under-neath his right arm with your left and grip on top of your right hand.

● Pull your elbows tight to his body, throttle his hand as if it were a motorcycle and squeeze your elbows together to tap.

Top wrist lock / neck lock combo

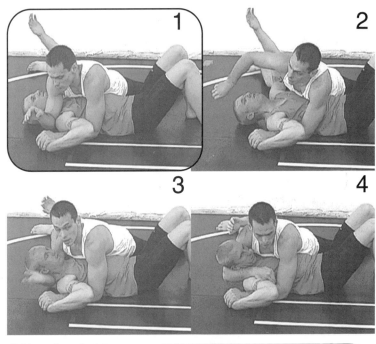

● You already have your top wrist lock set but for some reason can't solidify your tap. This will happen with a good and/or squirmy opponent.

● Retain his attacked hand with your hip-side hand (here the left).

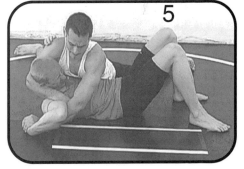

● Reach your head-side arm underneath his neck and hook your fingers deep into his right armpit.

● Straighten both your arms and arch your back to lever his neck from the mat and his wrist into the mat to tap.

Top wrist lock short arm scissors

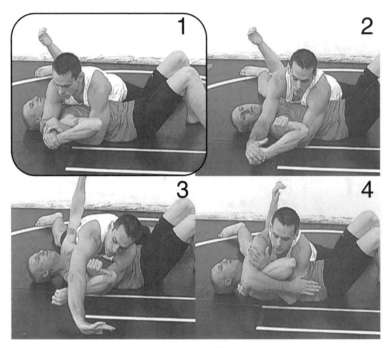

● You have your opponent in the top wrist lock position.
● He bursts his arm away from you and out to his right side.
● Follow his arm by hooking the crook of your head-side arm (here the right) over the top of his right wrist.

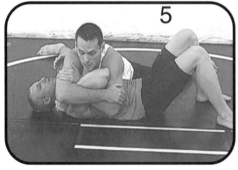

● Pull his arm back to you with the crook of your arm while inserting your left wrist tight into the crook of his right arm.
● To insert deeply, turn your left thumb toward the crook of his right arm and wedge your wrist tightly.
● With his arm trapped in this position, grip your triceps with both of your hands, squeeze your elbows tight together and arch your chest through his arms to tap.

143

Head and arm submissions

Hangman's drop

● From a right head and arm position, wrap the crook of your far arm (here the left arm) around the back of your opponent's head.

● Place the palm of your left hand on top of your right forearm in a reverse lever grip.

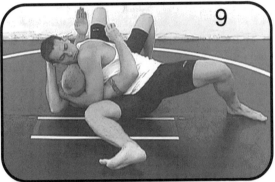

● Grip the back of your head with your right hand.

● Squeeze your elbows together tightly and lift his head from the mat.

● Sink your chest into him while sliding your hips toward the 12 o'clock position above his head to tap.

Figure-4 legs top wrist lock

● From a right head and arm position, capture his near arm (here his right arm) at the wrist with your left hand.

● Lean into his arm with all of your body weight and force it to the mat over the top of your bottom thigh (here the right thigh).

● His arm will now be bent. Trap his arm to the mat by placing your bottom leg calf over the top of his forearm.

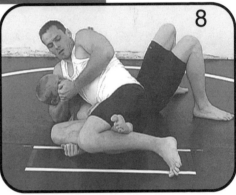

● Figure-4 your right foot behind your left knee.

● Grip your hands together palm-to-palm.

● Squeeze your knees together and lift his head from the mat and away from his trapped arm to tap.

Head and arm shin lock

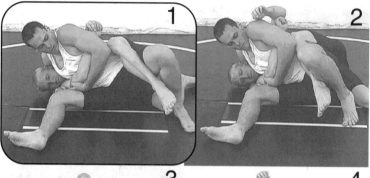

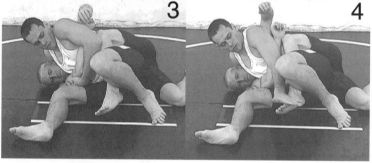

● From a right head and arm position your opponent has hooked his top foot (here his left foot) into your top hip (your left) in an escape effort.

● Do not remove the foot. Instead, squeeze your top knee toward your bottom knee bringing his hooked foot closer to you.

● Grab the toes of his now trapped foot with your top-side hand.

● Place the point of your top-side elbow into the inside of his shin just where muscle and bone converge.

● Squeeze your knees together, lever his toes toward your chest while digging your elbow into his shin to tap.

Top body hold submissions

Top wrist lock

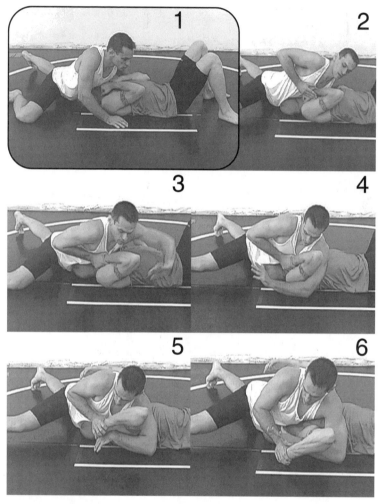

● If your opponent has his arms up and tight to his body to protect himself, seize an arm at the wrist (here you are controlling his right wrist with your right hand).

● Hip cut into his head with your left pelvis and switch your left forearm underneath his right triceps.

● Force his right wrist to the mat with all your body weight and grip your right hand with your left hand.

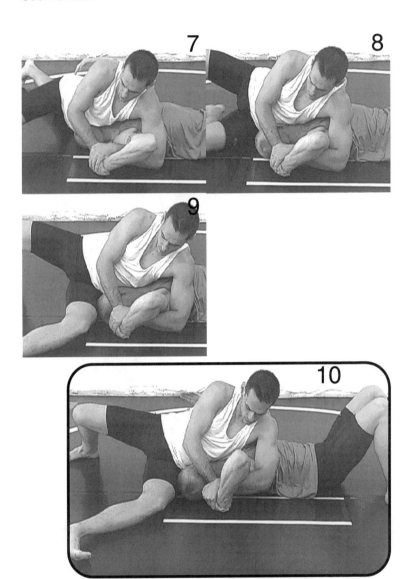

● Sit-out onto your left hip keeping weight on his head.

● Pull your elbows tight to his body, squeeze them together, and throttle the motorcycle to tap.

Overhooked top wrist lock

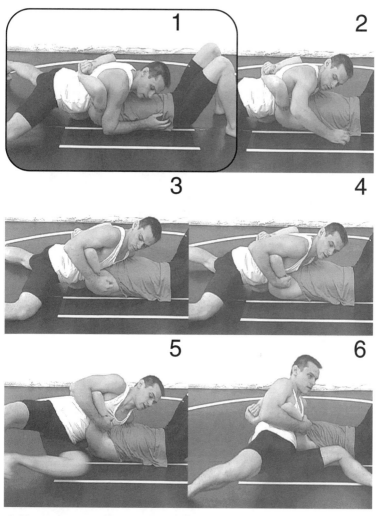

● Here your opponent has hugged you around the body in a bad strategical effort to halt your movement.
● Overhook one of his elbows with the crook of your same-side arm (here you use your right versus his right arm).
● Hug his arm tight to your body and sit-out on your left hip next to him being careful to keep weight on his head with your upper back and far arm.

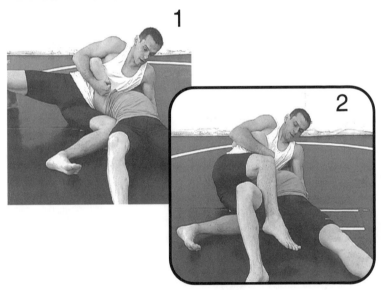

● Hook your outside leg (here your right) between his legs.
● Keep his hips down with your hooked leg, squeeze his body tight with your far arm, pull his trapped arm tight to your body. Arch your back to complete the tap.

Guard / bottom scissors submissions

Guillotine

● Overhook his head/neck with one of your arms (here the right).

● Cinch the overhooked arm around his neck and palm-to-palm grip your other hand.

● Pull your wrists toward your chin through his neck while pushing away with your legs to tap.

Another view ...

... and the grip ...

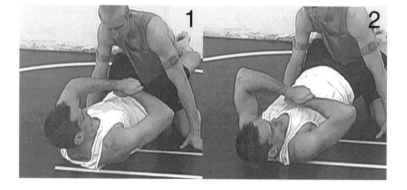

Arm bar

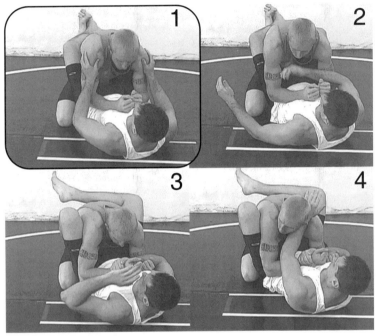

● When your opponent's arm is on your chest, grab his right hand with your right.

● Post your left foot in your opponent's right hip squeezing your left knee tight against his right elbow to prevent his freeing his arm.

● Put the outer blade of your left forearm into the left side of his neck.

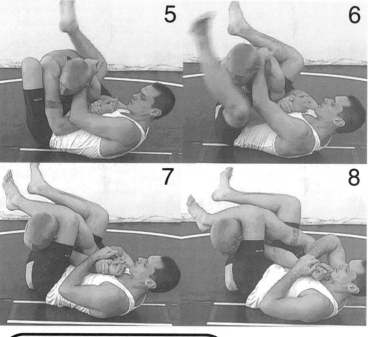

● Arch your hips and shoulders off the mat to create less drag as you perform the following spin.

● Use your posted foot and your left forearm in his neck to spin yourself perpendicular to your right.

● Put your left leg over his head and your hamstring in his face.

● Grip his captured arm with your left arm, pull him to you with your heels, keep his arm tight to your body with both of your arms. Squeeze your knees and arch your hips to tap.

Triangle choke

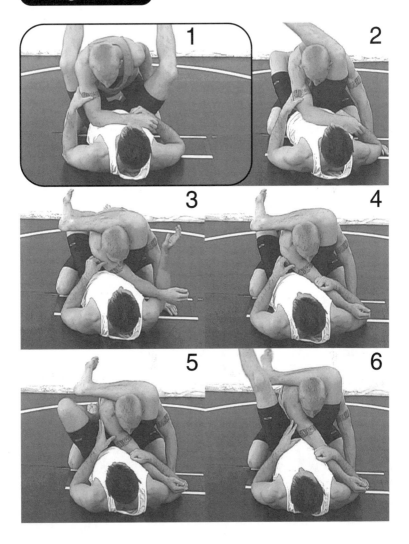

● Your opponent has one arm behind your hips and one arm on top of your hips (here the right arm is caught on top of the hips).

● Post your left foot onto his right hip, elevate your hips to his head and place your right leg on top of his left shoulder.

● Use your posted left foot to turn your body to your right perpendicular to your opponent.

● Figure-4 your legs.

● Pull his trapped right arm tight across his throat, squeeze your knees together, and arch your hips through his throat to tap.

● This is called a triangle choke because your right inner thigh, the back of your right calf and your opponent's right arm form a triangle when all the components are in position.

Double wrist lock

● Your opponent has his hands on the mat.

● Grab his posted right hand with your left hand.

● Release your leg grip and kick your left thigh into the back of his right upper arm to bring him into you.

5

● Overhook his right arm with your right arm. Reach under his forearm with your right to Figure-4 your arms.

6

● Regrip your legs, straighten his arm, twist his wrist and move his arm in an outward arc around his back toward his head to tap.

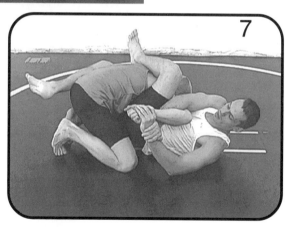

7

Coil lock

● From a double wrist lock position, step your left leg over his controlled right arm.

● Keep his forearm trapped across your abdomen throughout.

● Sit up into him facing the direction of his head.

5

6

● Grab his waist with your left hand to prevent his rolling out of the movement.

● Keeping his arm trapped with your forward body lean, get both your legs out to your right side and lean across his back at a 45-degree angle to tap.

7

8

Grapevine turnover

● You can have either the head and arm tie-up or a body lock on your opponent for this turnover.

● Release your leg grip and grapevine his legs by hooking your legs over the top of his and inserting your insteps under his ankles and spreading his legs wide.

● Pull his upper body high onto yours while stretching his lower body away with your legs.

5 ● Release one of your grapevines (here your right) and place your instep under his left thigh.

6 ● While dragging him up your body with your arms, kick your right leg toward the sky elevating his hips and turning him over to the mount where you can establish top control.

7

8

Inside guard submissions

Foot lock

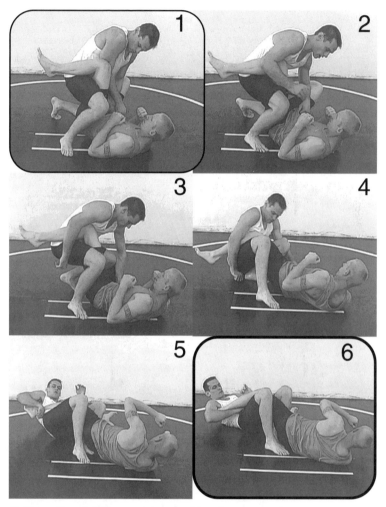

● From the right knee drive position be aware that your opponent may attempt to shove you back with his legs.

● When he does shove, retain the leg shelved on top of your knee-drive thigh by overhooking it with your right arm.

● As you fall back, fall to your left side and insert your left knee between his legs and step your right leg over the top of his left leg.

More views ...

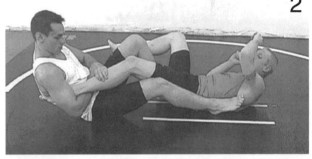

● Figure-4 grip your arms around his leg.

● Squeeze your knees together, extend away from him with your inserted left knee and arch your back. Straighten your Figure-4'd arms while turning the inside blade of your forearm toward his calf to tap.

Heel hook

● This is a continuation of the previous movement. Instead of overhooking his shelved leg on the fall back, pressure his leg tight to your right side keeping his toes under your armpit.

● All leg positions will be identical to the foot lock.

● Keeping his toes in your armpit, overhook his left heel with the inside of your right wrist.

● Clasp your hands in a palm-to-palm grip.

● Clamp your elbows tight to your side and squeeze your knees together. Arch your body back and to your left at a 45-degree angle taking his heel with you to tap.

Despite its name the heel hook actually attacks the knee joint and is a formidable move. Train carefully.

Half mount submission

Crown crush

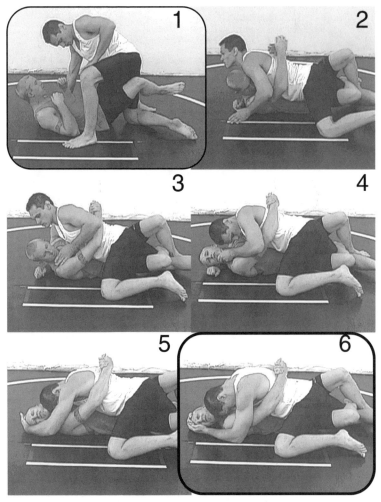

● Keep pressure on him so he can't attain full guard. Try lifting your caught leg off the mat taking his leg with you.

● Grip his head with both hands.

● Place the top of your head underneath his jaw and drive your body through his jaw while twisting his head to tap.

Back ride submissions

Sleeper

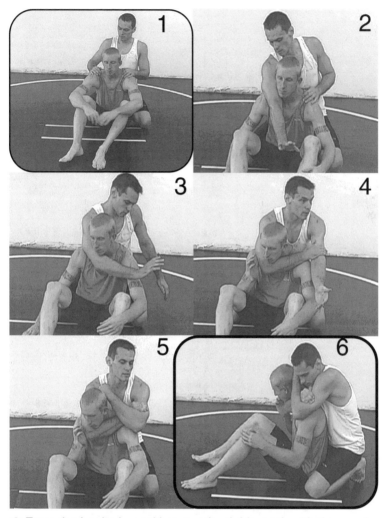

● From the hooks in position, overhook his neck with the crook of your right arm (the choke is shown in the seated position for a better view). ● Set your right palm onto your left biceps in a lever grip, placing your left hammer fist on the back of his head (the hammer fist is a stronger lever than the palm).
● Squeeze your elbows together while arching your chest through to tap.

Face lock

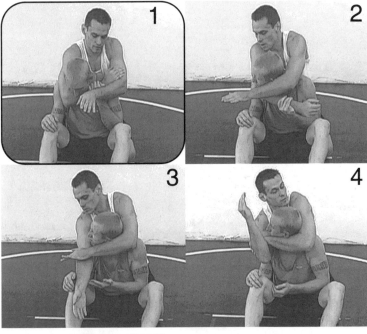

● Your opponent is guarding his neck.

● Bring your forearm across his face (this can be across the mouth, bridge of the nose or the eye sockets).

● Grab your left forearm in a reverse lever grip, squeeze your elbows together and arch your chest through him to tap.

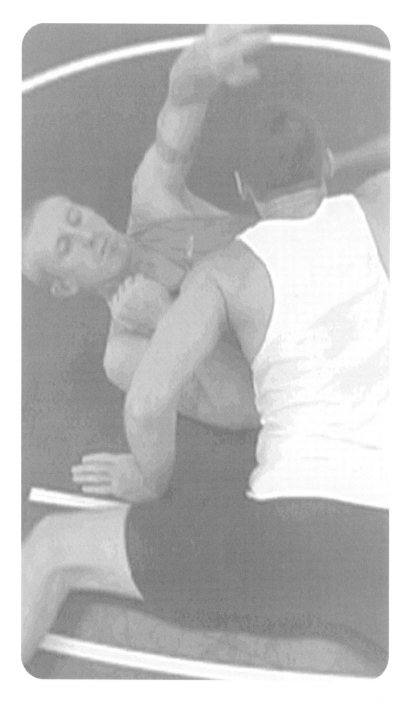

Head-to-head submissions

Front figure-4 choke

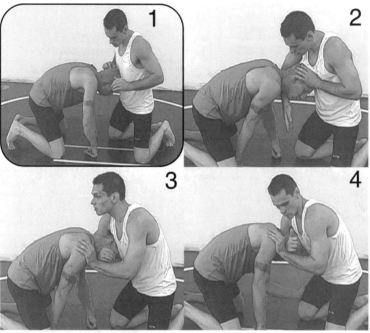

● Trap your opponent's head under your right armpit.
● Insert your right forearm (inner forearm blade facing up) into his throat.
● Post your left hand on his left shoulder.

● Figure-4 grip your left wrist with your right hand.
● Squeeze your elbows tight to your body, cut your right arm toward his throat, push away with your left hand and sink your base to tap.

Front face lock

● A variation of the previous move. Here your opponent has defended the choke by keeping his chin down.

● Perform everything as before, but here the right forearm is driving across the mouth and jaw.

Front head lock roll to cross-body neck crank

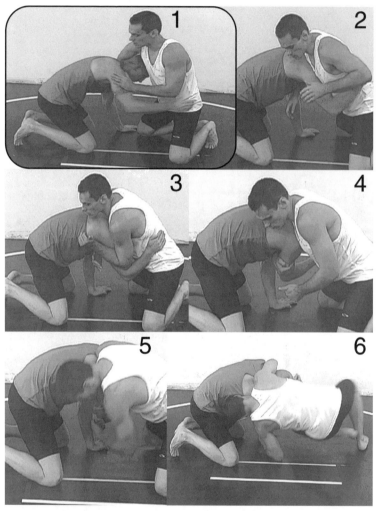

● You have your opponent's head under your right armpit.
● Force your left elbow into the crook of his right arm to pass his arm to your overhooked right hand.
● Grip his passed right arm tight at the triceps.
● Dip your head underneath and tight to the right side of his body while keeping your grip on his arm and head.

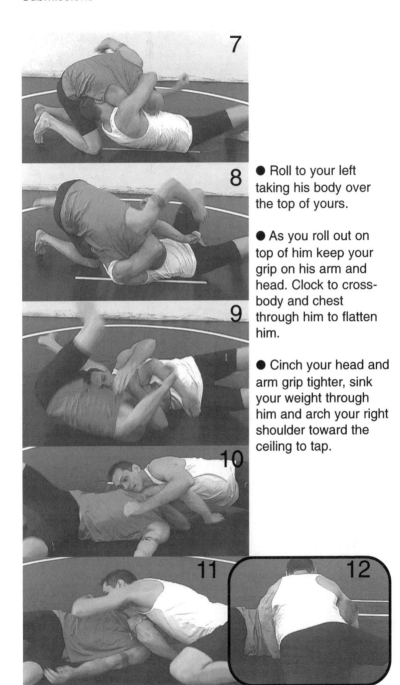

● Roll to your left taking his body over the top of yours.

● As you roll out on top of him keep your grip on his arm and head. Clock to cross-body and chest through him to flatten him.

● Cinch your head and arm grip tighter, sink your weight through him and arch your right shoulder toward the ceiling to tap.

Now you have a toolbox full of submissions for each of the positions. Work these on both the right and left sides of your body, paying close attention to the details of positioning, setups and, of course, the submissions themselves.

There are hundreds if not thousands more submissions, but these are basic moves that should serve very well in your grappling game.

Next we look at how to escape some of these moves and the ride positions we have covered.

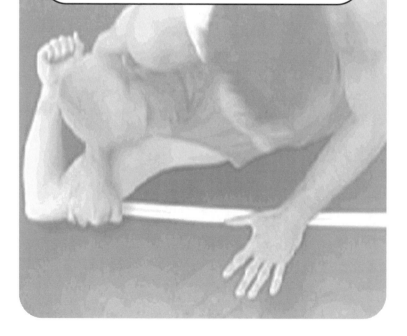

11 Escapes

Great escapes
Don't overlook the importance of this chapter.
While you are finding ways to ride and hook, so is
your opponent. That's what makes this sport like a
chess game. To be a successful player you've got to
be able to pull your fat from the fire many times.

A few thoughts on escapes:

1. Keep yourself in good position and there will be less chance that you will have a situation to escape from.

2. React immediately. The longer you wait under a ride or hook the more chance your opponent has to solidify his position.

3. Relax. Rule #2 Contradiction. If you are caught and locked down tight but aren't quite ready to tap ... relax. Sometimes it's this ability to exhibit grace under pressure or calm in the face of battle that frees up a little room for your body to work. If nothing else, relaxing allows your mind to work.

4. Chain escapes together like boxing combinations. Don't just shoot one move — keep moving and link them together making it tougher for your opponent to solidify his offense.

5. Tap. Don't be afraid to use the ultimate escape — the tap. If you are caught and you know it's going to hurt — tap. There's no shame in it. It's just a game. Come out from underneath and work on how you can prevent the same thing from happening in the future. It's just feedback. Relax.

We start with escapes from all of the basic positions. As we already know, if they can't ride you, they can't hook you. Let's make you unrideable.

Mount escapes

Grapes break

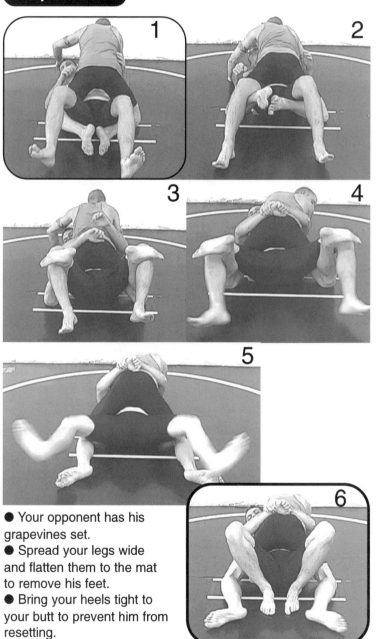

● Your opponent has his grapevines set.
● Spread your legs wide and flatten them to the mat to remove his feet.
● Bring your heels tight to your butt to prevent him from resetting.

Bridge and roll

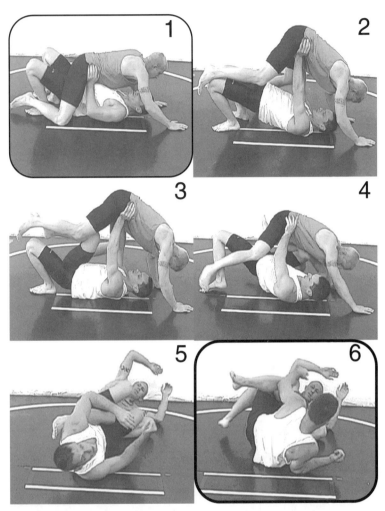

● An all-purpose escape when your legs are released from grapes. ● Place your palms into his hips, fingers facing out to prevent folded wrist locks. ● Bridge to the sky and use your hip movement to allow you to press his hips up and off you.
● Keeping his body on your locked arms, drop your hips and bring your right knee between his legs. ● Roll to your right side to remove him and/or throw your left leg over the top of his right leg to set a heel hook.

Elbow escape

● Bridge to your left side and insert your left elbow inside his right thigh. ● Shrimp to your right while bringing your left knee to meet your left elbow inside his right knee. ● Overhook his right leg with your left to place him in half guard. ● Bridge to your right side and repeat the previous steps to place your opponent in full guard.

Over the top

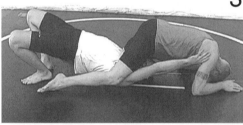

● Your opponent is riding high on you.

● Bridge deep and place your hands into his armpits as if you were going to military press your opponent over your head.

● While pressing him overhead, dig your heels into the mat and scoot your butt toward your feet.

● Jackknife your legs over the top of his back and hook your toes into his armpits replacing your hands.

6

7

8

● Extend your legs and back to push him off you while you roll out over a shoulder.

● This places you in a top position for either a scramble or a leg lock.

Cross-body escapes

Knee thru

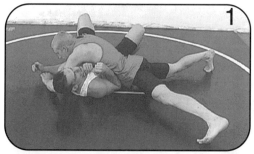

● Keep both your arms tight to your chest, hands up. It's as if you were in a horizontal boxing guard.

● Bridge deep and use your elbows to press into him to create room while turning into him.

● At the height of your bridge bring your near-knee out and around to attain either a full or half guard.

Bridge and roll

● Use whichever arm you can get free and hug his head-side arm tight to your body.
● Bridge deep and attempt to step your near-side leg over the top of your far-side leg turning away from your opponent.
● Once you step over, continue to hug him tight and walk toward your own head to roll him.

● You will now be in the top cross-body position.

Pressed arm bar

● If your opponent has his hip-side arm draped across the far side of your body, bridge deep. ● While bridging, wedge your far forearm in his throat to gain even more height. ● Quickly drop your bridge leaving your wedge in place and bring your outside leg around his head placing your hamstring over his neck.
● Grip his triceps with your outside hand, tighten your outside heel toward your butt and arch your hips to tap.

Head and arm escape

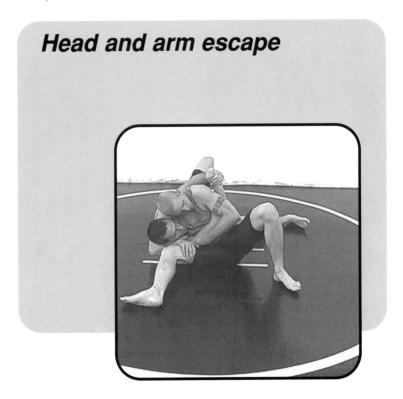

Bridge and roll

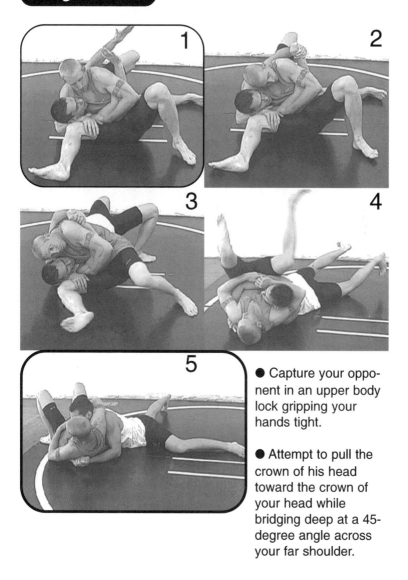

● Capture your opponent in an upper body lock gripping your hands tight.

● Attempt to pull the crown of his head toward the crown of your head while bridging deep at a 45-degree angle across your far shoulder.

Top body escapes

Over the top

● This is a variation of Over the top shown in the mount escapes section. ● Put both of your hands into your opponent's hips and press him away as if doing a horizontal military press. ● Dig your heels into the mat and slide your butt toward your heels. ● Jackknife your legs over the top and hook your toes into his hips. ● Use the purchase gained by your feet to pull your body out from underneath him. ● You will now be in a hooks in back ride.

Bottom inverted figure-4 leg choke

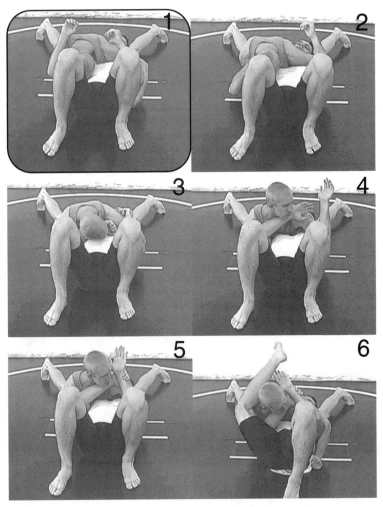

● Insert your right forearm, outside blade facing up, into his throat.

● Grip your left wrist and press his head up.

● Jackknife your right leg over the back of his head and grab your right ankle with your left hand.

● Keeping all of your grips intact, pull down on your ankle with your left hand while scissoring your right forearm and shin together to tap.

And the grip ...

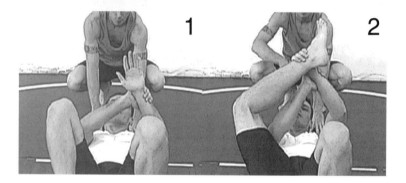

Guard / bottom scissors escapes

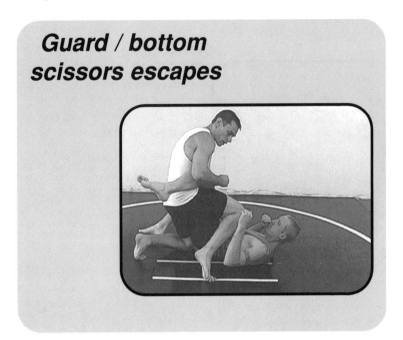

Near-knee pass

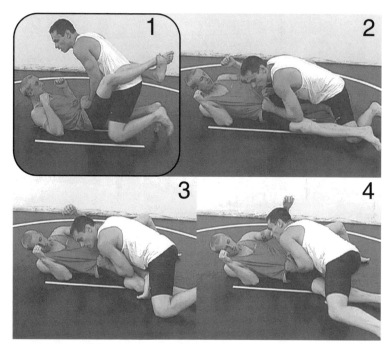

● Place your palms into his stomach at his waistband.

● Insert your elbows into the center of his femoral mass — the meatiest part of the thigh.

● Slide your right knee up and place it directly in his butt crack (sorry folks), while keeping your other knee on the mat at a 90-degree angle for base.

● Settle your weight through your elbows while stepping your back knee backward 45 degrees to split the legs.

● Once the legs are split, maintain the split with the elbows monitoring his inner thighs.

Another view ...

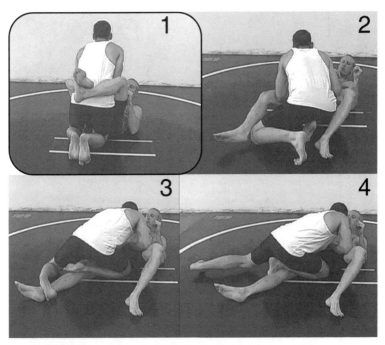

● The following steps must be strictly observed to prevent being reguarded, half-guarded and/or swept.

● Place your back knee over his leg leaving your back instep to the inside of his legs hooking over his ankle.

● Step your front leg instep over his leg while leaving your front knee on the mat to the inside of his legs.

● Step your back instep out and then your front knee out to attain cross-body position.

Sprawl slither

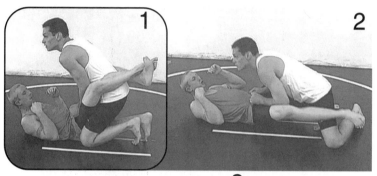

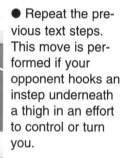

● Repeat the previous text steps. This move is performed if your opponent hooks an instep underneath a thigh in an effort to control or turn you.

● Leaving your elbows monitoring his inner thighs, sprawl your hips to the mat trapping his inserted instep to the mat.

● Slither your hips over the top of his inserted instep leg and gain cross-body position.

Pressure squat

● Repeat the first two steps of the near-knee pass.

● Step or jump to your feet being careful to keep your hips driving through his at all times.

● Keeping your elbows in his thighs, assume a semi-squat position with your feet based approximately one foot below his hips. Most of your weight will be on your toes as you drive your hips through (maintaining a hips-through position will help prevent your opponent having the ability to sweep you).

● From this semi-squat, the insides of your knees should be placed on the outside of your opponent's legs at midthigh level.

● Keep your hips-through pressure with elbows in and squeeze tight with the knees to break his leg grip.

● From here you can proceed with any of the previous or following passes.

Knee drive

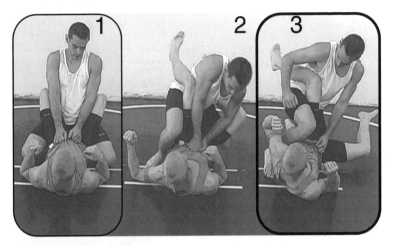

Another view ...

● Assume the pressure squat position.

● Force a knee (here the right knee) directly across his abs. Drive your knee through your man and into the mat.

● Once his legs break their grip (they will or his hips will lock) you can continue your drive to pass or set up leg locks.

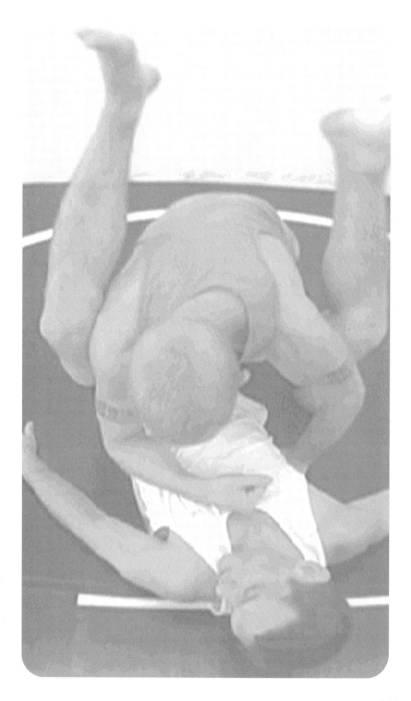

Open guard pass

Turning knee scissors / pinch

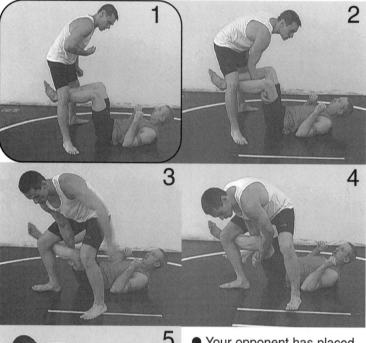

● Your opponent has placed his elevators under your thighs to control you. Your right arm underhooks his left knee.

● Step your left leg over his body and around to his left side.

● This step leaves your right forearm wedged behind his left knee, and his left foot is trapped behind your right calf.

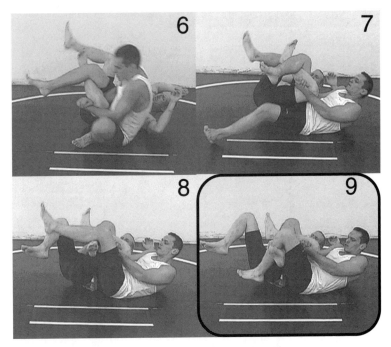

● Grab your hands in a palm-to-palm grip and Figure-4 your legs.

● Rock your body onto your upper shoulders, squeeze your knees together and pull your heels to your butt, while turning your forearm wedge toward your body to tap.

Back ride escapes

Crossed feet escape

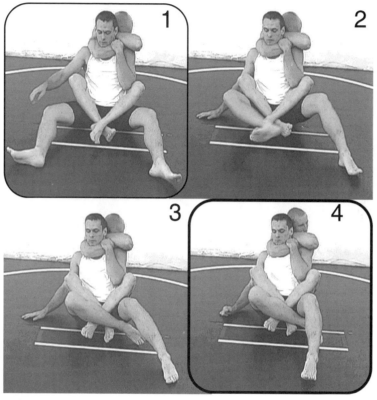

● Here your partner is on your back and you are belly-up. This is a crab ride.

● Your opponent has made the error of crossing his feet to keep you in the saddle.

● Cross your legs on top of his. Optimum placement is opposite leg crosses on top of his top leg. For example, if his left leg is crossed on top of his right, cross your right leg on top of his left and then cross your left on top of your right.

● Pull your ankles tight to your butt and arch your hips through his legs to tap.

Shin lock escape

● Here his feet aren't crossed and he hasn't gained complete control of your upper body.

● Overhook one or both feet at the toes and slide your hips toward his feet.

● Place your elbow(s) into the inside of his shin(s) at the juncture of bone and muscle.

● Pull his toes toward you and sink your elbows through his shins to tap.

Crab ride choke escape

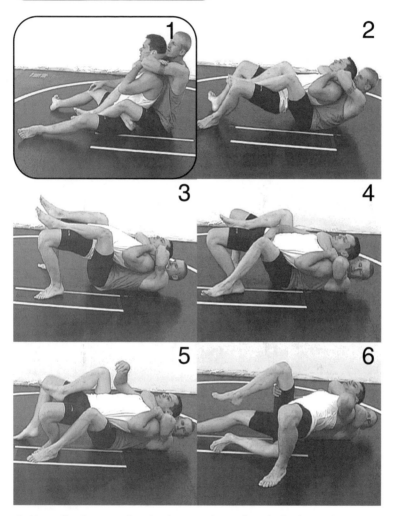

● Here the feet are hooked properly and a choke is sunk.
● Defend the choke by grabbing his right wrist with your left hand. Be sure to keep your left elbow tight to your body to prevent his levering your arm away. Only one arm is needed to defend a choke. A second hand placed at the crook of the arm or biceps is wasted effort.
● Arch/bridge into your opponent and use your free hand to remove his left hook.

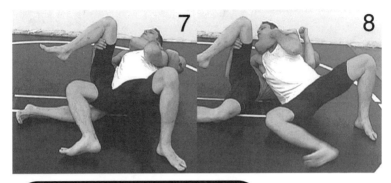

● Once the hook is removed, shrimp toward the hook-freed side. (Always work and shrimp toward the hand of the choking arm — not the crook of the arm.)

● Staying on your side and shrimping off his body will release you.

Belly down back ride escape

● Protect your neck by keeping your chin down and controlling the wrist of your opponent's choking arm.

● Keep your elbows tight to your side to keep him from controlling your wrists.

● Forcefully arch your legs toward the ceiling and attempt to put one knee behind the other (here the left behind the right).

● This removes his hooks. Bring your right knee under your hips.

● Keeping your hold on his choking wrist, bring your other knee underneath your hips.

● Use your free arm to remove any remaining hooks.

● Grip his choking arm with both hands, elevate your hips and pull him over the top to attain top position.

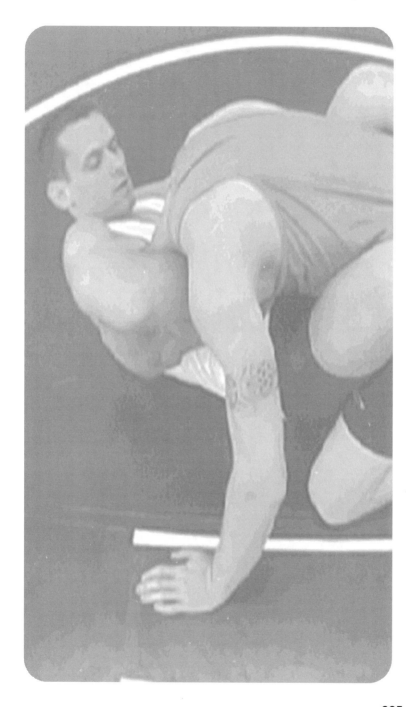

Submission escapes

Sleeve / naked choke escape

● This defense works against both the mounted or the guarded version of this submission. Use this defense while inside your opponent's guard.

● Grab one or both of his elbows and pull down hard. This removes the leverage he needs to choke.

Arm bar escape

● Use your far-side arm to shrug his hip-side leg over your head as you shrimp your hips toward his body and turn into him.

Short arm bar escape

● A short arm bar is a cross arm bar lacking the hip-side leg control. This leg is placed with the shin wedged into the back.

● Grip your hands in the 3-finger safety.

● Jackknife your legs up and over your outside shoulder at a 45-degree angle to bring yourself to your knees and out of the submission.

Top wrist lock escape

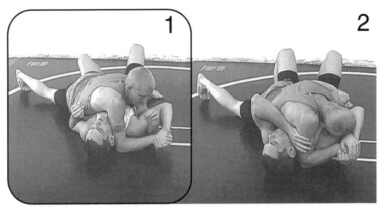

3

● Bridge deep toward your attacked arm while forcefully attempting to straighten it. Facilitate this movement by shoving hard into his near triceps with your free hand.

● This should compromise your opponent's base enough that he has to abandon the move to retain position. Next, shoot for a mount escape.

Guard guillotine defense

● Tuck your chin and turn your head toward his to keep him away from your chin.

● Overhook his wrist with your near-side hand and pull to release some pressure.

● Use your free hand to gouge the jugular notch (the indentation at the top of the sternum) to escape the choke.

Guard arm bar escape

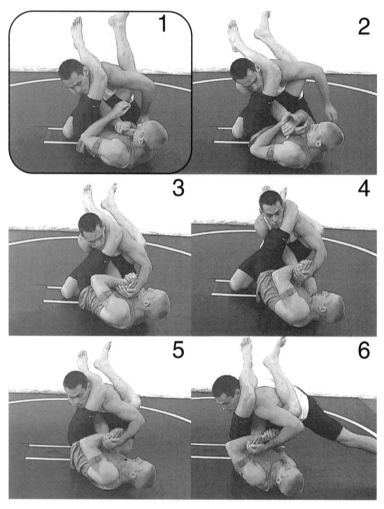

● Turn your attacked hand palm up.

● Cup the back of your attacked hand in your free hand and lever up. This stalemates his attack.

● Stack him knee to nose and turn toward his head away from your attacked arm to pull it out safely.

Belly down arm bar

● If you get turned from the previous move into the belly-down version of the arm bar, post your head on the mat and kick your legs over his body to remove your elbow from jeopardy and pull your arm out.

Foot lock escape

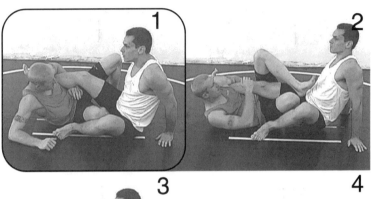

● As soon as your foot is caught, shove your leg deeper into his arms, straighten your leg, and pull your toes toward you. This moves his fulcrum further up your leg to less sensitive tissue and the toe point tightens the muscles over the underlying attacked nerves.

● Post your free foot on his butt and shove hard as you pull your attacked foot free.

Shoulder choke escape

● Open your captured hand and place your thumb into his biceps encircling your head. This will stalemate the choke.

● From here, bridge and roll toward your far-side to gain top position.

Triangle escape

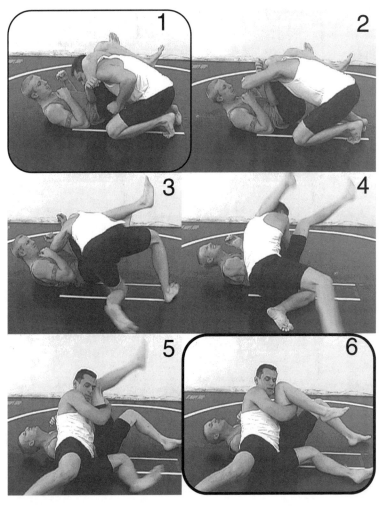

● Stay low and don't stack.

● Turn your head toward your caught shoulder as you perform a reverse sit-out — in effect pulling your head free.

● Turn into him to control him.

There you have it — an excellent vocabulary of escapes to keep you in the game. Next are some drills, both partner and solo, to hone your skills even more.

12 Drills

Grappling / NHB drills
There are many ways to mix up your training to add spice to an already exciting sport. The few featured are ones that you can play around with and change as you see fit. Most drills will fall into two broad categories: conditioning and technique cultivation. These two categories can be further broken down to solo and partner drills. The following drills combine the two categories with emphasis on technique cultivation.

SOLO DRILLS

Shadow wrestling

Boxers have shadow boxing, grapplers have shadow
wrestling. This is a great training tool when you lack a
partner or you are drilling a particular move or chain
of moves in order to engrave them into your system.
Shadow wrestling is getting on the mat and visualizing
an opponent in front of you. Shoot on your imaginary
opponent, thwart his shots, go for submissions, chain
submissions, chain escapes and engrave constant movement and flow.

The importance of shadow wrestling can not be over-
stated. Allow me to quote a well-known experiment in
which a college basketball team was divided into three
groups. The first group physically practiced their free
throws, the second group mentally rehearsed free
throws without actually shooting them, and the third
group used a mix of the two. The group that mixed the
two approaches showed a significant improvement
while the other two groups hovered in approximately
their same success percentage. Thus, we have a good
case for rolling by yourself. Visualize a partner in front
of you and make them as alive as you can. This mixed
with actual partner rolling time will greatly improve
your game.

Floor bag work

If you have a grappling dummy or a heavy bag, throw it
on the mat and go to work. Working the floor bag is
essentially shadow wrestling with a moveable object. It
takes the boxer's upright training apparatus to the horizontal to work positions — hips through, the ground

and pound game, gut wrenching, pressurizing and so on. Anything you can visualize in shadow wrestling can be used with the floor bag. Keep in mind these two drills are limited only by your imagination and desire to train.

PARTNER DRILLS

Wrestling chains
Grab a partner and this book or your notes from previous grappling sessions and work on specific movement drills. Do them until you are sure that they are part of your system. Be aware of precision of technique, both yours and your partner's. Pay attention to how each of your bodies move and learn to anticipate shifts in base and pressure. Paying attention in the drilling process makes reaction in sparring or competitive situations much easier.

Submission chains
Now add submissions. Play tit for tat on taps. You make a move and submit your partner with him resisting 50 to 60 percent. Then freeze your submission after his tap, ease up a little on the pressure and let him escape the movement and seek his own submission. Now you tap, he releases the pressure and you escape. Wrestling without endings is a great way to learn submissions and escapes while constantly moving.

Increase the difficulty of this drill by not repeating the same submission during the same session. This forces you to think and be on the lookout for numerous opportunities to submit. You can up the ante even further by making each other's previous submissions off limits. For example, if your opponent has already shot a top wrist lock from the mounted position, you can't use it even if you find yourself in a perfect position to do so. You have to think your way out of it and find an alternate move. Use the same limiting with escapes to increase your defensive skills.

Sparring
Sparring is great training and should not be used as an ego enhancer. To get the most from your training sessions, keep in mind that sparring is not the same as competition. Sure, you can have fun and roll with the intention to tap and not be tapped, but each sparring session should be an opportunity to learn more about your game and cultivate particular techniques or strategies.

When sparring, some days you will feel fresher than others. Sometimes you will be rolling with someone who has a great deal more experience than you and vice versa. It is convenient to have a standard of aggression so that each has an understanding of what is expected from the other. Try a 10-point system which arbitrarily assigns aggression a 10-point scale where 1 is a hug and 10 is full contact.

Before rolling with anyone it is advisable to agree on where on the scale you would like to train. I suggest that 5-6 is a good place to work on new techniques and strategies, 3-4 is good for beginners (although they will often shoot to 7-9), preparing for a match can be worked at around the 6-8 level, and 9-10 should be refereed closely and conducted with full safety gear.

Short offense
Wrestling starting from the knees prevents knocks on poorly matted surfaces and hard falls from takedowns. Good for beginners or light training.

From the feet
The match is started from the feet so takedowns are in. Be sure to agree on your 10-point scale and have adequate mat coverage before you begin.

NHB
All the strikes, shoots and hooks are incorporated. Agree on the 10-point system, have adequate mat coverage and all pertinent safety gear. It is also important to train with a good referee to assist in any ego flares.

Handicap training
This is a good way to cultivate particular aspects of your technique or strategy by forcefully limiting your opportunities. Handicap sparring should never rise beyond a 7 on the 10-point system. You can handicap in many ways and a few ideas are listed. Keep in mind you can play handicapped against a non-handicapped player or you can each be assigned a handicap. Please remember the following suggestions are to get you started. Use your imagination!

● Takedowns versus takedown defense
● Striking versus takedowns
● Standing versus a grounded opponent
● Position playing only (you try to pin your man for five seconds but no submissions) versus submissions
● Only arm locks allowed
● Only leg locks allowed

- Only neck attacks allowed
- Only the right limbs available for submission
- Only the left limbs available for submission
- Right leg/left arm submissions only
- Left leg/right arm submissions
- Feet tied together
- No arm wrestling (arms tied to the sides with a gi belt)
- One arm wrestling (an arm is tied inside the gi belt)
- Blindfold wrestling

Bull in the ring
Here's a grueling sparring game to play when you have multiple training partners. One individual has to fight each training partner in succession. Example: There are six folks in attendance. You pick one to fight the other five, one after the other. This is great conditioner and will teach you a lot about using technique over strength to conserve energy. Each partner may be grappled to a tap or there may be timed wrestling periods of, say, two minutes duration.

King of the hill
This is another continuous sparring game ideal for multiple partners. Two start and wrestle to a tap. The victor remains and fights the next in line. They wrestle to a tap and so on. By playing this way a more skilled opponent may indeed get more mat time, but if you play long enough fatigue will become a factor and make even the most skilled tappable.

Battle royale

All against all. Exactly what it sounds like. Every man
for himself. Everyone starts wrestling at once. As soon
as you tap your man, move on and tap someone else,
even if he is in the middle of another match. You continue until there is only one player remaining.

These ideas should spice up your training. Keep in
mind first and foremost the safety lecture. Have fun,
train hard, leave the egos at the door and learn.

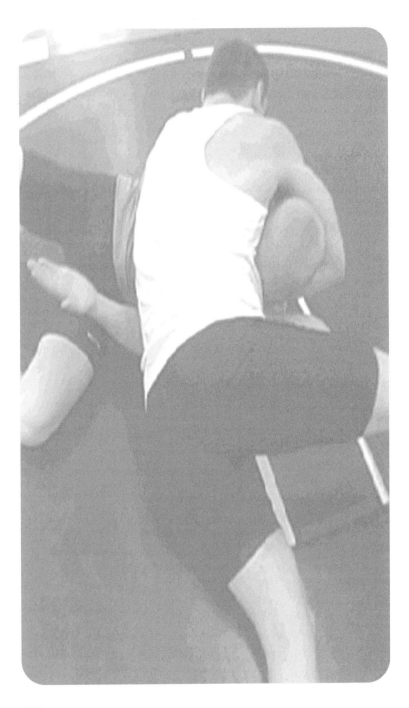

NHB / submission wrestling resources

This is a growing game with knowledgeable enthusiasts. Ten years ago there were few reputable resources. Today there are many. This list is not comprehensive. Omission of any resource is not condemnation or lack of respect, just author's oversight.

Equipment

Everlast
718-993-0100

Fairtex
www.fairtex.com

Ringside
1-877-4-BOXING
www.ringside.com

Magazines

Grappling

Fight Sport
fightsportmag.com

Full Contact Fighter
fcfighter.com

Books

Boxer's Start-Up:
A Beginner's Guide to Boxing
by Doug Werner

Brazilian Jiu-Jitsu:
The Master Text
by Gene "Aranha" Simco

The Fighter's Notebook
by Kirik Jenness and David Roy

No Holds Barred: Evolution
by Clyde Gentry III

Video instruction

Paladin Press
paladin-press.com
Includes videos by Mark
Hatmaker

Panther Productions
panthervideos.com

Threat Response Solutions
trsdirect.com
Includes videos by Mark
Hatmaker

World Martial Arts
groundfighter.com

Extreme Self-Protection
extremeselfprotection.com
Mark Hatmaker's Web site

Events

The Ultimate Fighting
Championships
ufc.tv

Pride
pridefc.com

King of the Cage
kingofthecage.com

Universal Combat Challenge
ucczone.ca/

Pancrase
so-net.ne.jp/pancrase

IFC
ifc-usa.com

IVC
valetudo.com

Web sites

sherdog.com

extremeselfprotection.com
Mark Hatmaker

mmafighter.com

bjj.prg

adcombat.com

Where to learn
These resources provide you with
learning materials and/or opportunities. Also check your local
yellow pages under martial arts or
karate.

Allow me a moment for self-pro-
motion. You can log onto
www.extremeselfprotection.com
for my own Web site. You will find
even more instructional material,
training videos, links to other
resources, and a long-distance
instruction service to get you well
on your way to meeting your
training goals.

Please drop by and take a look.
Send me an e-mail if you have any
questions or comments.
mhatmaker@hotmail.com

Index

Mark Hatmaker has 23 years experience in the martial arts (boxing, wrestling, Jiu-jitsu and Muay Thai) including 18 years of instructing. He is a highly regarded coach of professional and amateur fighters, law enforcement officials and security personnel. Mark is founder of Extreme Self Protection (ESP), a research body that compiles, analyzes and teaches the most effective unarmed combat methods known. ESP holds numerous seminars throughout the country each year, including the prestigious Karate College / Martial Arts Universities in Radford, Virginia. He has produced several instructional videos including *Escapes From Impossible Holds* (3 volume set), *Ground Zero (Real World Survival Grappling)*, *Brutal Submissions* and *Guard Submissions*. He lives in Knoxville, Tennessee.

Doug Werner is the author or co-author of 15 sport and fitness instructional guides including the Start-Up Sports® series. He lives in San Diego, California.

Order more fighting books and tapes
www.extremeselfprotection.com

Find out about all the sport / fitness instructional guides from Tracks Publishing
www.startupsports.com or call **800-443-3570**